Mission Possible!

by

Insight Publishing

I0040984

EBOOK EDITION

Copyright © 2003 Insight Publishing

Published in the United States by:

Insight Publishing Company
707 West Main Street, Suite 5
Sevierville, TN 37862
800-987-7771
www.insightpublishing.com

A Message from the Publisher

Some ideas simply get better with time. *Mission Possible!* Began as a promotional idea for professional speakers who were trying to expand their careers. Sharing the pages of a book with famous personalities like Stephen Covey, Mark Victor Hansen, and Bruce Jenner was a simple, but innovative strategy. One year later, *Mission Possible!* has taken on a life of its own and proven to be much more than a promotional tool.

What has become crystal clear to all of us who help publish *Mission Possible!* is that our contributing authors all have vibrant, life-changing messages. These professional speakers, trainers, and consultants are living "success stories." The counsel they give is based on real-world experience, not theory. And because each chapter is a transcribed interview, readers can have a personal encounter with each author, making the ideas presented even more relevant and entertaining.

Mission Possible! should be required reading for anyone wanting to grow and succeed. Regardless of the challenges you face in your career or personal life, the ideas, insights, and strategies presented by these dynamic personalities will make a difference for you. Don't miss a chapter in this exciting edition of *Mission Possible!* and watch for new editions coming soon!

Interviews Conducted by:
David E. Wright, President
International Speakers Network

Chapter One – Jack Canfield

-

David E. Wright (Wright)

Today we are talking to Jack Canfield. You probably know him as the founder and co-creator of the *New York Times* number one best-selling *Chicken Soup for the Soul* book series, which currently has thirty-five titles and fifty-three million copies in print in over thirty-two languages. Jack's background includes a B.A. from Harvard, a master's degree from the University of Massachusetts, and an honorary doctorate from the University of Santa Monica. He has been a high school and university teacher, a workshop facilitator, a psychotherapist, and for the past twenty-five years a leading authority in the area of self-esteem and personal development.

Jack Canfield, welcome to *Mission Possible!*

Jack Canfield (Canfield)

Thank you, David. It's great to be with you.

Wright

I talked with Mark Victor Hansen a few days ago. He gave you full credit for coming up with the idea of the *Chicken Soup* series. Obviously, it's made you an internationally known personality. Other than recognition, has the series changed you personally—and if so, how?

Canfield

I would say that it has, and I think in a couple of ways. Number one, I read stories all day long of people who've overcome what would feel like insurmountable obstacles. For example, we just did a book, *Chicken Soup for the Unsinkable Soul.* There's a story in there about a single mother with three daughters. She got a disease and had to have both of her hands and both of her feet amputated. She got prosthetic devices and was able to learn how to use them so she could cook, drive the car, brush her daughters' hair, get a job, etc. I read that and I think, "What would I ever have to complain and whine and moan about?" So I think at one level it's just given me a great sense of gratitude and appreciation for everything I have, made me less irritable about the little things. I think the other thing that's happened for me, personally, is that my sphere of influence has changed. By that I mean I got asked, for example, a couple of years ago to be the keynote speaker to the Women's Congressional Caucus; these are all the women in Congress, governors, and lieutenant governors in America. I said, "What do you want me to talk about, what topic?" They said, "Whatever you think we need to know to be better legislators." And I thought, "Wow, they want *me* to tell them about what laws they should be making and what would make a better culture?" Well, that wouldn't have happened if our books hadn't come out and I hadn't become famous. I think I get to play with people at a higher level and have more influence in the world. That's important to me, because my life purpose is inspiring and empowering people to live their highest vision so the world works for everybody, and I get to do that on a much bigger level than when I was just a high school teacher back in Chicago.

Wright

I think one of the powerful components of that book series is that you can read a positive story in just a few minutes, come back and revisit it. I know my daughter, who is thirteen now, has three of the books, and she just reads them interchangeably. Sometimes I'll go into her bedroom and she'll be reading one of them and crying. Other times she'll be laughing, so they really are chicken soup for the soul, aren't they?

Canfield

They really are. In fact, we have four books in the *Teenage Soul* series now and a new one coming out at the end of this year. I was talking to one of my sons—I have a son who's eleven, and he has a twelve-year-old friend who's a girl. We have a new book called *Chicken Soup for the Teenage Soul on Tough Stuff.* It's all about dealing with parents' divorces, teachers who don't understand you, boyfriends who drink and drive, and stuff like that, and I asked her, "Why do you like this book?" (It's our most popular book among teens right now.) And she said, "You know, whenever I'm feeling down I read it, and it makes me cry, and I feel better. Some of the stories make me laugh and some of the stories make me feel more responsible for my life. But, basically, I just feel like I'm not alone."

One of the people that I work with recently said that the books are like a support group between the covers of a book, to hear other people's experiences and realize you're not the only one going through something.

Wright

I have been booking speakers for twelve years. I read that you have a speakers bureau with the *Chicken Soup* series authors.

Canfield

Yes, it's called the Souperspeakers Bureau.

Wright

Are those the people who have contributed to your books?

Canfield

Yes.

Wright

That's a great idea.

Canfield

Yes, it's wonderful, and we get a lot of wonderful speakers who are absolutely inspirational and motivational and can deliver a good content. It's nice to know that we're able to do that, to bring messages of hope and inspiration to people.

Wright

Jack, with our *Mission Possible!* talk show and publication, we're trying to encourage people in our audience to be better, to live better, and to be more fulfilled by listening to the examples of our guests. Is there anything or anyone in your life that has made a difference for you and helped you to become a better person?

Canfield

Yes, and we could do ten shows just on that. I'm influenced by people all the time. If I were to go way back, I'd have to say one of the key influences in my life was Jesse Jackson when he was still a minister in Chicago. I was teaching in an all-black high school there, and I went to Jesse Jackson's church with a friend one time. What happened for me was that I saw somebody with a vision. This was before Martin Luther King was killed, and Jesse was one of the lieutenants in his organization. I just saw people trying to make the world work better for a certain segment of the population. I was inspired by that kind of visionary belief that it's possible to make change.

Then, later, John F. Kennedy was a hero of mine. I was very much inspired by him. And later, a therapist by the name of Robert Resnick, whom I had for two years, taught me a little formula called $E+R=O$ that stands for Events+Response=Outcome. He said, "If you don't like your outcomes, quit blaming the events and start changing your responses." One of his favorite phrases was, "If the grass on the other side of the fence looks greener, start watering your own lawn more." I think it helped me get off any kind of self-pity I might have had because I had parents who were alcoholics and that whole number. It's very easy to blame them for your life not working. They weren't real successful or rich, but I was surrounded by people who were, and I felt like, "What if I'd had parents like they had? I could have been a lot better." He just got me off that whole notion and made me realize the hand you were dealt is the hand you've got to play, and you've got to take responsibility for who you are and quit complaining and blaming others and get on with your life. That was a turning point for me.

I'd say the last person who really affected me big time was a guy named W. Clement Stone, who was a self-made multimillionaire in Chicago. He taught me that success is not a four-letter word; it's nothing to be ashamed of, and you ought to go for it. He said, "The best thing you can do for the poor is not be one of them. Be a model for what it is to live a successful life." So I learned from him the principles of success, and that's what I've been teaching now for the last—almost thirty years.

Wright
He was the entrepreneur in the insurance industry, wasn't he?

Canfield
He was. He had Combined Insurance, and when I worked for him he was worth six hundred million dollars—and that was before the dot-com millionaires came along in Silicon Valley. He just knew more about success. He was a good friend of Napoleon Hill, who wrote *Think and Grow Rich,* and he was a fabulous mentor. I really learned a lot from him.

Wright
I miss some of the men that I listened to when I was a young salesman coming up, and he was one of them. Napoleon Hill was

another one, and Dr. Peale—all of their writings made me who I am today. I'm glad that I got that opportunity.

Canfield
One speaker whose name you probably will remember, Charlie Tremendous Jones, says, "Who we are is a result of the books we read and the people we hang out with." I think that's so true, and that's why I tell people, "If you want to have high self-esteem, hang out with people with high self-esteem. If you want to be more spiritual, hang out with spiritual people." We're always telling our children, "Don't hang out with those kids." The reason we don't want them to is that we know how influential people are with each other. I think we need to give ourselves the same advice. Who are we hanging out with? We can hang out with them in books, cassette tapes, CDs, radio shows like yours, and in person.

Wright
One of my favorites was a fellow named Bill Gove from Florida. I talked with him about three or four years ago, and he's retired now. His mind is still as quick as it ever was. I thought he was one of the greatest speakers I had ever heard.

Canfield
He had one of the greatest voices too.

Wright
What do you think makes up a great mentor? In other words, are there characteristics that mentors seem to have in common?

Canfield
I think there are two obvious ones. I think they have to have, one, the time to do it, and two, the willingness to do it. And then, three, I think they need to be someone who is doing something you want to do. W. Clement Stone used to tell me, "If you want to be rich, hang out with rich people. Watch what they do, eat what they eat, dress the way they dress. Try it on." It wasn't, like, give up your authentic self, but it was that they probably have habits that you don't have. Study them; study the people who are already like you. I always ask salespeople in an organization, "Who are the top two or three in your organization?" I tell them to start taking them out to lunch and dinner and for a drink and find out what they do. Ask them, "What's your secret?" Nine

times out of ten they'll be willing to tell you. It goes back to what we said earlier about asking. I'll go into corporations and say, "Who are the top ten people?" They'll tell me, and I'll say, "Did you ever ask them what they do differently from you?" They'll say "No." "Why not?" "Well, they might not want to tell me." "How do you know? Did you ever ask them? All they can do is say no. You'll be no worse off than you are now." So I think with mentors you just look at people who seem to be living the life you want to live, achieving the results you want to achieve. We tell them in our book that when you approach a mentor they're probably busy and successful and so they haven't got a lot of time. Just say, "Can I talk to you for ten minutes every month?" If I know it's only going to be ten minutes, I'll probably say yes. The neat thing is, if I like you, I'll always give you more than ten minutes, but that ten minutes gets me in the door.

Wright

When you consider the choices that you've made down through the years, has faith played an important role in your life?

Canfield

Yes, totally. I believe deeply that I was born with a purpose, a mission. As I told you earlier, it's to inspire and empower people to live their highest vision in such a way that the whole world works for everybody. I always had faith that I was doing God's work and that I was being supported by God and spiritual energies that are available to me. I've always taken risks. I've made the commitment of my time and my resources to do the things that I feel driven to do. For example, when it became clear I was supposed to put together a book of stories and didn't have a title, which eventually became *Chicken Soup for the Soul,* half of my staff said, "You're crazy. You can't make any money. Books don't sell that well. That's a dumb title. You need to be out there doing speeches. Quit writing. Let's do more marketing for your talks." And here we are, over sixty-eight million copies of our books sold now. But I felt divinely inspired. It was like divine obsession. I trusted that if I did what I was hearing in my inner voices in my heart—I call it not my will, but thy will—then the resources would be there to support me. It's the old thing: if you'll jump, we'll build wings on the way down. That's been my belief all along. I believe that I am part of the universal flow of spiritual energy, and so faith in that is very critical to my life and faith in God.

Wright

In the future, are there any more Jack Canfield books authored singularly?

Canfield

Yes, I'm working on two books right now. One's called $E+R=O$, which is that little formula I told you about earlier. I just feel I want to get that out there, because every time I give a speech, when I talk about that, the whole room gets so that you could hear a pin drop; it gets silent. You can tell that people are really getting value. Then I'm going to do a series of books on the principles of success. I've got about a hundred and fifty of them that I've identified over the years. I have a book down the road I want to do called *No More Put- Downs,* which is a book probably aimed mostly at parents, teachers, and managers. There's a culture we have now of put-down humor. Whether it's *Married With Children* or *All in the Family,* there's that characteristic of macho, put-down humor. There's research now that's showing how bad it is for kids' self-esteem, co-workers, and athletes when the coaches do it, so I want to get that message out there as well.

Wright

It's really not that funny, is it?

Canfield

No, we'll laugh it off because we don't want to look like we're a wimp, but underneath we're hurt. The research now shows that you're better off breaking a child's bones than you are breaking his spirit. A bone will heal much more quickly than his emotional spirit will.

Wright

I remember recently reading a survey where people listed the top five people who had influenced them in their lives. I've tried it on a couple of groups at church and other places. In my case, and also in the survey, it's running that about three out of the top five are always teachers. I wonder if that's going to be the same in the next decade.

Canfield

I think probably it will, because as children we're at our most formative years. We actually spend more time with our teachers than we do with our parents. Research shows that the average parent interacts verbally with each of their children only about eight and a half minutes a day. Yet at school they're interacting with their teacher for anywhere from six to eight hours, depending on how long their school day is—and then there are coaches, chorus directors, and so forth. So I think that in almost everybody's life there's been that one teacher who loved you as a human being—not just as a subject matter, some person they were supposed to fill full of history and English— but believed in you and inspired you. Les Brown is one of the great motivational speakers in the world. If it hadn't been for one teacher who said, "I think you can do more than be in a special ed class; I think you're the one," he'd probably still be cutting grass in the median strips of highways in Florida instead of being a $35,000-per-talk speaker.

Wright

I had a conversation one time with Les when he was talking about a wonderful teacher who discovered that he was dyslexic. Everybody else called him dumb, but one lady just took him under her wing and had him tested. His entire life changed because of her interest in him.

Canfield

I'm on the board of advisors of the Dyslexic Awareness Resource Center here in Santa Barbara. The reason is, I taught high school with a lot of kids who were called "at-risk"—kids who would end up in gangs and so forth. What we found over and over was that about seventy-eight percent of all kids in the juvenile detention centers in Chicago were kids who had learning disabilities—primarily dyslexia, but there were others as well. They were never diagnosed, and they weren't doing well in school, so they'd drop out. As soon as you drop out of school, you become subject to the influence of gangs and other kinds of criminal and drug-linked activities. If they had just diagnosed these kids earlier—and there are a lot of really good programs that can teach dyslexics to read and so forth—then we'd get rid of half of the juvenile crime in America.

Wright

My wife is a teacher, and she brings home stories that are heartbreaking, about parents not being as concerned about their children as they used to be, or at least not as helpful as they used to be. Did you find that to be a problem when you were teaching?

Canfield

It depends on what kind of district you're in. If it's a poor district, the parents could be drugged out, on alcohol, not available, basically. If you're in a really high-rent district, the parents might not be available because they're both working and coming home tired, they're jet-setters, or they're working late at the office because they're workaholics. Sometimes it just legitimately takes two paychecks to pay the rent anymore. I find that the majority of parents care, but often they don't know what to do. They don't know how to discipline their children. They don't know how to help them with their homework. They're not passing on skills that they never got. Unfortunately, the trend tends to be like a chain letter. The people with the least amount of skills tend to have the most number of children. The other thing is, you get crack babies. In Los Angeles, one out of every ten babies born is a crack baby.

Wright

That's unbelievable!

Canfield

Yes, and another statistic is fifty percent of kids, by the time they're twelve years old, have started experimenting with alcohol. I see a lot of that in the Bible Belt. It's not the big city, urban designer drugs, but you get a lot of alcoholism. Another thing you get, unfortunately, is a lot of—let's call it familial violence, a lot of kids getting beat up and hit, parents who drink and then explode, and, as we talked about earlier, child abuse and sexual abuse. You see a lot of that.

Wright

Most people are fascinated by the TV shows about being a survivor. What has been the greatest comeback that you have made from adversity in your career or in your life?

Canfield

You know, it's funny; I don't think I've had a lot of major failures and setbacks where I had to start over. My life's been on kind of an intentional curve. But I do have a lot of challenges. Mark and I are always setting goals that challenge us, and we always say, "The purpose of setting a really big goal is not so that you can achieve it so much, but it's who you become in the process of achieving it." A friend of mine, Jim Rose, says, "You want to set goals big enough so that in the process of achieving them you become someone worth being." I think that to be a millionaire is nice, but so what? People make money, they lose it. People get the big houses, they burn down, or Silicon Valley goes belly up and all of a sudden they don't have a big house anymore. But who you became in the process of learning how to do that can never be taken away from you. So what we do is, we constantly put big challenges in front of us.

We have a book coming out in a month called *Chicken Soup for the Teacher's Soul.* You'll have to be sure to get a copy for your wife. I was a teacher, and I was a teacher trainer for years. But in the last seven years, because of the success of the *Chicken Soup* books, I haven't been in the education world that much, so I've got to go out and relearn how to market to that world. I met with a superintendent of schools. I met with a guy named Jason Dorsey, who's one of the number one consultants in the world in that area. I found out who has the best-selling book in that area. I sat down with his wife for a day and talked about her marketing approaches.

So I believe that if you face any kind of adversity, whether you lose your job, or your husband dies, or you get divorced, or you're in an accident like Christopher Reeve and become paralyzed, or whatever, you simply do what you have to do. You find out who's already handled this and how they did it. Then you find out either from their book or from their tape or by talking to them or interviewing them, and you get the support you need to get through it. Whether it's a counselor in your church, or whether you go on a retreat or read the Bible, you do something that gives you the support you need to get to the other end, and you have to know what the end is that you want to have. Do you want to be remarried? Do you just want to have a job and be a single mom? What is it? If you reach out and ask for support, I think people really like to help other people. They're not always available, because sometimes they're going through it. But there's always someone with a helping hand. Often I think we let our pride get in the way. We let our stubbornness get in the way. We let our belief in how the world should be get in our way instead of dealing with how the world is. When we get that out of the way, then we can start doing that which we need to do to get where we need to go.

Wright

Do you still provide self-esteem resources and training to social workers, welfare recipients, and H&R people? Is it through The Foundation for Self-Esteem?

Canfield

Yes, I have in Culver City (which is part of Los Angeles) a foundation called The Foundation for Self-Esteem. It's run by a man named Larry Price. We've developed a number of programs, one that everyone on welfare in California has to go through, called the GOALS program, and we've been successful in lowering the amount of time people stay in this program for retraining and getting people off the welfare rolls. We've also got that program in San Quentin prison. It's in a number of prerelease programs for prisons. We're now developing a program called Y.E.S., which is Youth Empowerment Seminars, using the same principles. We teach what we call the ten steps to success. It's all the kind of stuff that you and I have been talking about on this show and that are in the book, like the power of focus and so forth. We've made it a video-based program that can be taught to anybody, at any reading level, and get them motivated and excited about life and taking responsibility and doing the things they need to do. It's a good example of what we were just talking about. People on welfare are facing adversity, and it's just a way that shows them what they need to do to get off.

Wright

Are there other states involved in things like that?

Canfield

Yes, we've got our program in thirty-five states, but in most other states it's not a mandatory program like it is in California. We've had over 430,000 people go through this program. We get letters all the time from people saying, "I wish I'd learned this in school." We got a letter from a prisoner the other day saying that if he'd learned these principles before he was eighteen, he wouldn't have had to do what he did that allowed him to go to prison. We had another guy up in Oregon who had read *Chicken Soup for the Soul* that someone had sent him in prison. He said, "If I had read stories like this when I was a kid, or they had been read to me, I wouldn't be here either."

Wright

I was reading some material about you in preparation for this interview. I can remember when I was in junior high school there was a man who was a coach at the school. Most of us really respected him. Of course, I kept up with him all the way through my college days. When I was in my late thirties, I met him one day and I still called him "Coach." It was such a term of endearment and respect. When I was reading the material, it said that you are best described as "an understanding, compelling, empowering and compassionate coach." Is that a title that you're proud of?

Canfield

Yes, I think so. I consider myself a success coach, or a life effectiveness coach, not a football coach or a track coach. But as I said earlier, we all need coaches. I could not have played football in high school or track and basketball if I hadn't had a coach to teach me what to do. Unfortunately for the American school system, someone did a research study recently that showed that less than ten percent of the American high schools ever teach anything about goal setting, how to create a balanced life, communication skills, conflict management skills, or how to resolve problems. I always tell people that no one got divorced because they didn't memorize the seven causes of the Civil War or the five exports of Brazil. The reason we get divorced is that we don't have the basic life skills we need to either choose correctly as a partner or to manage conflicts. Conflicts come up and people just start pulling away from each other and don't share their feelings. There's an emotional and social education that we never get, and, unfortunately, people have to go out and avail themselves of that education through books, seminars, tapes, and by listening to shows like yours to make up for what should have been taught to us in school. I will tell you that most of the people who are listening to this show are not using the trigonometry and calculus they learned in high school. But they *are* needing to know how to talk to their kids, how to deal with someone when they're angry, how to develop a good habit in place of a bad one. I always wished there had been a class in high school called Education of the Self, and that you'd have to study "self" science as well as physical science. Maybe someday we'll have that.

Wright

I can remember being in a room of about three or four hundred people one time, and most of them, I assume, were college graduates.

The speaker on the platform asked the question, "How many of you, either in grades 1 through 12 or in college, have walked through a door where the title of the class was Decision Making?" Not one person could hold up their hand. He made the same point that you're making. He went on to say that not only are we not taught to make decisions, the people who love us most protect us from making decisions. Those things are important.

Canfield

Think about money management. The average American will have anywhere from a million to two million dollars go through their hands in a lifetime. That's if you're only making $25,000 to $50,000 a year. If you're making $100,000 a year, you can multiply that by four. So what happens is that most of us have never had any training in school or college about how to manage our finances, how to plan for retirement. The big secret that all the really successful people know is that from the age of about twenty or twenty-five, if you put away one-tenth of your income every month, by the time you're sixty-three you'll have a million dollars in a stock market account. But most of us start out when we're about fifty, then we'd have to live to be a hundred to have that, so it's a little late. But it's a crime that we don't teach things like decision making. We make decisions all day long, yet a lot of the big ones, like who to marry, what job to take, what church to go to, we're not getting much guidance on.

Wright

If you could have a platform and tell our audience something that you feel would help or encourage them, what would you say?

Canfield

I'd say, number one, believe in yourself, believe in your dreams, and trust your feelings. I think too many people are trained like this: When they're little kids and they're mad at their daddy, they're told, "You're not mad at your daddy." They say, "Gee, I thought I was." Or you say, "That's going to hurt," and the doctor says, "No, it's not," and then he gives you the shot and it hurts. He says, "See, that didn't hurt, did it?" You start not to trust yourself. Or you say to your mom, "Are you upset?" and your mom says "No" when she really is. So you stop learning to trust your perception. I tell the story over and over. There are hundreds of people I've met who've come from upper-class families where they make big incomes, and the dad's a doctor, and the kid wants to be a mechanic and work in an auto shop because that's what he loves. The family says, "That's beneath us. You can't do that." So the kid ends up being an anesthesiologist killing three people because he's not paying attention. What he really wants to do is tinker with cars. I tell people you've got to trust your own feelings, your own motivations, what turns you on, what you want to do, what makes you feel good, and quit worrying about what other people say, think, or want for you. Decide what you want for yourself, and then do what you need to do to go about getting it. It takes work. I tell people that I read a book a week, minimum, and at the end of a year I've read fifty-two books. We're talking about professional books, books on self-help, finances, psychology, parenting, and so forth. If you do that, at the end of ten years you will have read five hundred and twenty books. That puts you in the top one percent of people knowing stuff in this country. But most people are spending their time watching TV.

W. Clement Stone told me when I went to work for him, "I want you to cut out one hour a day of TV." I said, "Okay, what do I do with it?" He said, "Read." He told me what kind of stuff to read. He said, "At the end of a year you'll have spent 365 hours reading. Divide that by a forty-hour work week and that's nine and a half weeks of education every year." I thought, "Wow, that's two months." It's like going back to summer school. As a result of that, I have close to eight thousand books in my library. The reason I'm on your show instead of someone else is that people like me and you and Jim Roane and Les Brown read a lot. We listen to tapes and we go to those seminars. That's why we're the people with the information. I always say that your raise becomes effective when you do. You'll become more effective as you gain more skills, more insight, and more knowledge.

Wright

Jack, I have watched your career for over a decade, and your accomplishments are just outstanding. But your humanitarian efforts are really what impress me. I think that you're doing great things, not only in California but all over the country.

Canfield

It's true. In addition to all of the work we do, we have all of our books. We pick one to three charities, and we've given away over six million dollars in the last eight years, along with our publisher who matches every penny we give away. We've planted over a million trees in Yosemite National Park. We've bought hundreds of thousands of cataract operations in Third World countries. We've contributed to the Red Cross, the Humane Society, and on it goes. It feels like a real blessing to be able to make that kind of a contribution in the world.

Wright
Well, we are out of time. I could talk to you all afternoon.

Canfield
Thank you. It was great talking to you as well.

Wright
Today we have been talking to Jack Canfield, the founder and co-creator of the *Chicken Soup for the Soul* book series, which currently has thirty-five titles, and I'll have to update this. It was fifty-three million; how many has it been now, Jack?

Canfield
We're almost up to seventy-eight million. We have a book coming out in just a couple of weeks called *Chicken Soup for the Soul of America*. It's all stories that grew out of September 11, and it's a real healing book for our nation. I would encourage your listeners to get themselves a copy and share it with their families.

Wright
I will stand in line to get one of those. Thank you so much being on *Mission Possible!*

About the Author

In addition to being the founder and co-creator of Chicken Soup for the Soul®, Jack is the founder of Self-Esteem Seminars, which trains entrepreneurs, educators, corporate leaders, and employees how to accelerate the achievement of their personal and professional goals. Jack is also the founder of the Foundation for Self-Esteem, located in Culver City, California, which provides self-esteem resources and training to social workers, welfare recipients, and human resource professionals.

Jack Canfield
Self-Esteem Seminars
P.O. Box 30880
Santa Barbara, CA 93130
(805) 563-2935, ext. 20
www.jackcanfield.com

Chapter Two – Carol Ann Small

-

David Wright (Wright)

Today we're talking to Carol Ann Small, founder and CEO of Laughter with a Lesson. Carol Ann is a motivational speaker, trainer, and humor consultant who imparts wisdom with a twist of comedy. She is also managing editor of *Small Talk* humor newsletter. A professional member of the National Speakers Association and the Association for Applied and Therapeutic Humor, Carol Ann offers her clients a unique perspective on the benefits of laughter and finding humor in the workplace. She received her degree in speech communication and performing arts from Emerson College in Boston. Small has been featured in *Health Magazine, Employment Times*, and *Strathmore's Who's Who*. Her corporate clients include Aetna, Avon, Digital Equipment Corporation, Dunkin' Donuts, Fidelity Investments, Hewlett-Packard, Beth Israel Deaconess Medical Center, and numerous other health-care organizations.

Carol Ann Small, welcome to *Mission Possible!*

Carol Ann Small (Small)

Good morning!

Wright

Carol Ann, I was fascinated by one of your seminar topics, *If I Only Go Around Once in Life, Then Why Am I So Dizzy?* Do you really feel that stress is creating major problems for companies?

Small

Everyone is so stressed out that they are not performing at their optimum level of productivity. That's why I focus my work on Laughter with a Lesson. I like to work with organizations that want to boost morale, improve productivity, and create a happy work environment. We are all so overcommitted, and everyone is just taking themselves too seriously and not really enjoying their lives anymore. Remember the good old days when advances in technology meant upgrading to a four-slice toaster?

Wright

Do I ever! I have a fourteen-year-old. I could write a book on overcommitment!

Small

Young people are even more over-committed than adults. I have a niece who pencils me in her day planner for the week. If I'm lucky, she fits me in between piano and Jamboree!

Wright

In your experience, do most corporations exhibit a certain attitude in terms of either being lighthearted or all business?

Small

It really travels from the top down. I think the CEO and top managers really determine what kind of environment people are allowed to work in. It's just amazing. You could visit a hospital and it could be quite serious. You could visit another health-care facility around the block and it could be more lighthearted. It's not that you're not doing your job well, but it's so much easier to go to work when you enjoy the people you work with—you can actually have a laugh once in a while. We spend so much of our daily lives working that we really should find appropriate ways to enjoy ourselves too.

Wright

So the management team sets the whole style?

Small

Yes, management gives people permission regarding whether it's acceptable if they can have a little fun at work, whenever that might be appropriate. There's a time and a place for everything, but I have found employees far more motivated when they have work that they can enjoy and co-workers who maintain a positive attitude.

Wright

What advice or instruction would you give to people who are experiencing stress right now?

Small

First, just two simple words: Lighten up! Everyone is so serious. Take a good look at your current challenges and ask yourself how important this will be a month from now. It's the total accumulation of the small stresses. Sometimes it's not the major stressors, because we can get support for handling those; but it's the everyday little disappointments and stresses. I suggest that people carry a small notebook for a week and write down every little thing, person, and place that annoys you. You will be amazed at the end of the week how those little stresses add up to enormous stress. What can you change and what can't you change?

Wright

You talk about creating a humor environment. What exactly does that mean?

Small

I tell my audiences to create a humor environment at home and at work—even something simple, such as having a little library on your desk containing humorous materials, a volume of cartoons, a squeezable stress ball. Plan one fun activity each week, especially at work. Take a five-minute "humor break." When people get stressed out, they usually reach for coffee or sugar. I suggest going for a walk, taking a break from the stress, and attempting to focus on something more positive for just five minutes. Soon you will be refreshed and ready to return to work again. People oftentimes forget to schedule anything fun in their daily routine, such as lunch with a friend who makes you laugh. We schedule time for the dentist, doctor, or mechanic, but we forget to include a fun activity in our daily scheduling.

Wright

Does exercise play an important role? The reason I ask is that I know an insurance company that built a walking path around the entire block, and all their people go out and walk at a certain time every day.

Small

Walking is extremely beneficial. Studies have shown that exercise can really relieve depression. When you're depressed, the last thing you're motivated to do is go exercise, but it's amazing how exercise releases the endorphins into your brain and gives you that natural "high." I friend of mine said she joined a fitness club last year and actually gained a few pounds. Nobody told her that when you're standing on the treadmill you have to turn it on!

If you're sitting at a computer all day and you're locked into a work environment, it's really good to get outside of the office—look at nature, refocus, get a new perspective, and then come back. Some people do not give themselves that break. They just work straight through, and they wonder why at five or six o'clock they're so stressed; it's because they never took a break. If they do have a break, they're far more productive in the afternoon versus that sluggish, droopy feeling that comes on at three. Take a walk around the block; it's better for you than a cup of coffee!

Wright
So if you're at the office all day and you stress out and then get into your car and go home, you take all of that stress to the greatest place in the world. And then what happens at home?

Small
If you take it home, then naturally your mate or your children might feel the brunt of your negative attitude. People always talk about how important it is for there to be some kind of meaningful transition from work to home. Sometimes people go to the gym. When my husband would come home from work, I used to follow him around and chat. He's a quiet guy and that was not the correct thing to do. I didn't realize he really needed that half-hour transition—just like he didn't realize my idea of gourmet cooking was a couple of burritos from Taco Bell!

Wright
You do a lot of work with corporations in team building. How do you include the use of humor in team building?

Small
It's been said that laughter is the shortest distance between two people. It also creates a bond. If a corporation has a teambuilding issue, and if there are some activities offered, sometimes you develop a new relationship or a new friendship. Then, when you're working on a team, it feels as if you're working with a friend towards a common goal versus all strangers who want different goals. If we have co-workers we feel are our friends, we'll be inspired to work harder towards that goal.

Wright

There are so many different styles of personalities in corporations. Can humor bridge that gap?

Small

People can have different types of humor. One program I teach in communication identifies the specific behavioral styles. Everyone is a combination, but we're predominately one or two. It's really important to communicate with people in their preferred style. You might have someone who's very analytical, concise, to-the-point, and that's how they prefer to communicate. And then you may have a chatterbox like myself who likes to begin with, "Hi, how was your day?" and after pleasantries get down to business. What we tend to do is communicate with others in our own style; so if a chatterbox like myself goes to a bottom-line person and socializes too much, that's not going to work. When I'm working with someone who's very focused, perhaps the head of a company, and they just want the bottom-line answer, that's how I communicate with them. I get to the point; I tell them what I can do and it's over. With someone else I'm perhaps more social, because they're social. We're taught to treat people the way we want to be treated; we really need to treat them the way they want to be treated.

Wright

When you said that about the atmosphere coming from the top, I remembered one time I booked a speaker for an engineering company that was having a dinner for husbands and wives. They wanted a technical speaker. I said, "Isn't this a Valentine's Day dinner? Why don't you let me get you a humorist?" I thought the lady was going to drop the phone, but I talked her into it. It was the greatest meeting the company ever had; she got many complimentary letters from the people who attended. Sometimes you just assume that someone who's analytical—an engineer, an accountant—doesn't have a good sense of humor. That's not a safe assumption, is it?

Small

Not at all. I'm married to an analytical, concise person, but he does have a sense of what is humorous. Sometimes we have a slightly different sense of humor. Some people show it more than others. Women tend to show it a little more than men, unless the men are really outgoing. There's a delayed reaction sometimes if I'm presenting to a predominately corporate male audience, because sometimes they're analyzing what's going on and looking at the CEO to see how the CEO reacts, to see if they have permission to laugh at that particular moment. It used to throw my timing off, because I'd say something and think, Oh, all right, I should move on—and then I'd hear "Ha, ha, ha," but delayed about thirty seconds. That's why it's so important for the top person to be involved in the project, to give people that kind of permission. It's important as a speaker. I always send pre-program questionnaires and interview employees in advance to really get to know the group. They might call me with one idea in mind, but after I've conducted all of my research, we realize together that something else might be better. I think it's about people staying open to suggestions.

Wright

Down through the years I've gone to many, many conferences with two, three, four thousand people in a room, and I've always come away thinking that all the good things the people said about the conference had to do with how they felt more than what they had learned. They just felt good about the whole meeting, and generally there was a lot of humor going on.

Small

Even if you're a technical speaker, it's important to have a sense of humor. There's an old joke in the speaking business that says you only have to have humor if you want to get paid. It doesn't matter what you're teaching the audience; a sense of humor works wonders for breaking up the technical aspect of the day. I spoke yesterday, and the corporation had technical topics all day. I was the first person at the end of the day to comedically inspire them before dinner. People need a break, and it doesn't matter what the topic is. When you have a sense of humor and you relate humorously with the audience, you bond with them more and they will listen. We've all been through college classes with the stoic professor who was brilliant but was monotone and boring and it put us right to sleep. Humor livens up the pace and keeps the audience awake, alert, and interested.

Wright

While preparing for this interview, I read that employers ranked attitude at the top of their priority list. You stated that you have methods and techniques that transform negative attitudes into positive one. Can you explain how this happens?

Small

I teach a program called *Adventures in Attitude.* Attitude is really all a matter of perception. We have a choice to make every day regarding attitude, how we're going to perceive events in our lives. It's really how we react to the situation. You can take two different people in the same situation, and one will react in a positive way and one in a negative way. We're all going to have stresses and unfortunate things happen, and the trick I have found that helps is to remain focused on the solution. If we just keep looking at the problem and it seems there's no way out, what we need to do is get out of the problem and into the solution. I even have a friend that I call when I'm stuck in the problem. Everyone should have someone they can call. Joe will say to me, "All right, I hear you. That's the problem; what is the solution?" You feel better even if you take one small step towards the solution. Attitude really helps with our coping skills. We can all use an attitude adjustment at one time or another in our daily lives. You can also learn from positive people. I've admired people who are very uplifting and motivating and positive. We learn from them. The more you surround yourself with friends, family, and co-workers who are like that, you will automatically encounter more of them.

Wright

It's odd that you would have a workshop titled *Adventures in Attitude.* Years ago I took a life-changing, seventy-two hour workshop titled *Adventures in Attitude,* where I learned something that has stayed with me all these years: It's not what people do or say to me, it's how I react that really counts. I've never forgotten that. I think it was a Carlson Learning program.

Small

That's the program that I teach. This program has been around for many years, and as you said, it has positively changed people's lives. I've been studying attitude adjustment and motivation for twenty years, and a few years ago I got involved with this and thought, There's always something new, and we can always benefit. I went in thinking this would be a good thing to teach people. I thought, I'm pretty positive most of the time, and I've read books for twenty years; there probably won't be too many new things for me to learn. But it's just amazing that there's always something new to discover—we can always benefit.

Wright

Carol Ann, with our *Mission Possible!* talk show and book, we're trying to encourage people in our audience to be better, live better, and be more fulfilled by listening to the examples of our guests. Is there anything or anyone in your life that has made the difference for you and inspired you to become a better person?

Small

There have been several people along my path. First of all, my family has a wonderful sense of humor. In a house filled with storytellers, I had to quickly cultivate a sharp wit to keep up with the dinner table conversation and be heard. There have been several other people along my path.

The next one I can think of is my piano teacher, Winnie, who lived downstairs from my parents. We became friends when I was five and I think she was about sixty. Winnie was not a surrogate grandmother; she was just my pal. She was the first person who said to me, "You can do anything you want!" It's funny; sometimes if it isn't a family member but a friend, you can be more accepting of the praise and the encouragement. My piano teacher was the first one, and there have been other supporters along the way.

Dr. Ken Crannell, a wonderful speech teacher at Emerson College, was also very inspiring to me.

I've wanted to express my own comedic side ever since I saw Carol Burnett having so much fun on her variety show. I've also studied many motivational speakers over the years. I longed to get up on stage and explore my own creativity, but I had a lot of limiting beliefs and fears that held me back for a while. I guess you could say I was an introverted extrovert. I firmly believe that it's important to surround yourself with people who truly believe in you and have them handy for those days when you don't believe in yourself.

Wright

What particular qualities do you think all the great mentors share?

Small

I think a mentor needs to be someone that you trust, who tactfully tells you when you may be going off track. You want someone who is truthful with you, but they also need to be supportive, and they need to know and understand your behavioral style. Some people want to be bottom-line. For me, I need a more encouraging person, someone I know who has my best interests at heart. It's wonderful to find those people in life who absolutely love you and want you to succeed. It's satisfying and fulfilling to watch people that I've mentored achieve their goals. When they achieve their goals, I'm as excited as they are, and I think that's really important.

Wright

So the most important thing would actually be helpful participation in another person's progression. If you're genuinely thrilled by the success of others, then you're basically participating in that joy.

Small

Yes! It doubles your joy. It takes you out of your own self-centeredness, because we can all be a bit self-absorbed at times. It's wonderful to be around people who are so inspiring or motivating. Again, I think of my family, my piano teacher, my husband, Brian, and my best friend, Joe. These are some individuals along the way who have been wonderful and incredibly supportive.

Wright

Most people are fascinated with these new television shows concerned with being the ultimate survivor. What has been the single greatest comeback that you've made from adversity in your career or in your life?

Small

I like to say that I'm the "twenty-year overnight success story." It took a lot of years, but ever since I was eight years old and my mother and I watched Carol Burnett on television, I was convinced that the ability to get audiences laughing is truly a gift from God. I never thought I would actually be doing anything with humor, but I always kept my eye on the goal. Although I had my share of traditional jobs— I was a court stenographer, then I kiddingly say I woke up—I remained captivated by comedy and humorously uplifting situations. So it took me a long time to get to where I wanted to be, but it's just amazing that when you keep focusing on what you want, little by little it will come to you. I knew more conventional jobs were not my true calling, so I just kept focusing on what I truly wanted. Like everyone else, I had stressors, financial constraints, health issues, tragedies in life, and it's easy to get distracted and be thrown off track. I kept following my heart's desire. It took a while, but pursuing my authentic self was absolutely the best thing I ever did.

Wright

I was reading an Associated Press report just this morning about the Carol Burnett reunion show that aired a few months ago. It was one of the highest-rated shows on television, and CBS has promised to repeat it. There was an entire article on how people wished that shows like that would appear today . . . and, as you said, it has positively changed people's lives.

Small

It's really nice to enjoy programming that you can actually watch with your children—shows that aren't brimming over with foul language or adult situations. Burnett has always been a great inspiration to me. When I do a workshop and my contact tells me that they'd like some humor after dinner, I bring in some colorful characters much like those delightfully zany ones that Carol Burnett did on her classic television show. What a gift Carol Burnett and Jonathan Winters have to make us all laugh and forget our daily challenges! Can you imagine the millions of people who have said that as they're tuning in with their children? How many prime-time television shows can you actually watch with your children now and not be embarrassed by the colorful language?

Wright

To answer your question, I cannot watch prime-time television with my fourteen-year-old daughter. I have to watch her kind of television. She is a loyal Disney Channel viewer, but we honestly cannot watch any of the other prime-time programming together.

Small

It's embarrassing, isn't it? It's wonderful that at least with Disney or TV Land there's something decent to watch. All the great shows that we grew up with, like *The Carol Burnett Show, I Love Lucy,* and *The Mary Tyler Moore Show,* are terrifically entertaining and appropriate for a nine- or ten-year-old to see.

Wright

When you consider the choices that you've made through the years, has faith played an important role in your life?

Small

In retrospect, I can say yes. I call it the inner prompting. For years, before I would fall asleep at night, there would always be this little internal voice whispering, "You're not doing anything with humor . . . you need to be doing something with comedy." When I was toiling in these very traditional jobs, I knew I wasn't following my true calling. Sometimes we don't trust our own instincts, but it's just amazing what can happen when you do pay attention to the urgings of those little all-knowing voices! Sometimes I think God sends you messages through other people. I heard Dr. Robert Schuller II talking the other day about how it's important to pay close attention when people keep telling you that you're gifted at something or really talented in a particular area of your life. How many times do people have to tell you? There's that joke about a person drowning and God sends a boat, a plane, and a helicopter, and the person doesn't climb aboard any of them and drowns. When it's coming from everyone around you, does God have to send you a lightning bolt? I used to say that until I actually experienced a lightning storm. Now I say, "Please . . . just send me a fax next time!"

Wright

In the very beginning, were you an introverted person? You described yourself earlier as an "introverted extrovert."

Small

I was probably somewhat insecure as a kid. I loved humor. I had a weight problem and acne and what I refer to as "childhood challenges." We all had those hurdles, I guess. Looking back, I remember doing parodies, playing the piano with a friend of mine, and we would sing. If I was around certain people, the more theatrically outrageous aspects of my personality would come out. Now as an adult, I'm taking singing lessons and I very much want to incorporate parodies into my corporate presentations. People have been telling me for years, "You should do parodies! You should sing!"

Recognizing my own fears has been important in trying to overcome some of these blocks. That's been another major breakthrough. In the past I would say, "Oh, I'm not singing in front of people!" and now that's a whole new venue. That's why it's good to keep new goals and new passions alive. It's important to have a motivating force that makes you excited about waking up in the morning . . . besides Krispy Kremes, crullers, and coffee.

Wright

I'm going to date myself here, but I remember taking a music history class at the university. There was one point in time when we studied Spike Jones. Research revealed that his band had some of the greatest musicians that were living at that time. Here he was playing all humor, all for laughs. If you go back and listen to that music, it was all very tasteful but very funny. I don't know if you know who Spike Jones was?

Small

I have to confess that I don't know, but I'm writing his name down now. See, you learn something new every day!

Wright

If you could have a platform and tell your audience something you feel would help or encourage them, what would you say to them?

Small

I'd say, "Write down your heart's fondest desires and focus intently upon them every day." It's just like creating a contract with yourself. It's so easy just to daydream about things you'd like to accomplish, and then you get distracted in life and start putting things off. But there's something about having a written contract, a goal. Put it in your desk, in your pocketbook, your briefcase, your car. Focus on it every day. When you look at it, reflect on how you're doing in terms of making steady progress: Am I doing something on a daily basis to contribute toward that goal? I remember hearing somebody say, "If you spend thirty minutes a day focusing on your goal, you'll become an expert in that area in five years." So make sure that you set aside personal time each day. If you find yourself brushing your teeth at a red light, you might want to revise your day planner.

Wright

That is great advice. I've spent years in ruts myself, and it's not at all pleasant when you glance back and say, Why did I do that for so long?

Small

We've all done that. I've had some health concerns over the years that were caused by too much stress, by not following my creative aspirations, by working at jobs that were not correct matches for me. It caused me a great deal of stress, and as a result I developed adrenal stress syndrome. I was just worn out and exhausted all the time. If it wasn't for the door on my office, like many CEOs I wouldn't have gotten any sleep at all! It's a good thing they never took me up on my suggestion to install a Craftmatic adjustable bed in the employee lounge—I might have remained shackled to my cubicle.

Now my life is very different. When I'm having a challenging day, I call up my humor buddies, who say, "Stop focusing on the problem and focus on the solution!" I've heard time and again about the miraculous transformations that can occur when you articulate your goals—particularly when you write them down. They manifest far more quickly that way. A year later, a month later—it's truly amazing when you look back and you can clearly see all the wonderful things that you've created for yourself.

Wright

Carol Ann, I really appreciate your being with us on *Mission Possible!*

Today we have been talking with Carol Ann Small, founder and CEO of Laughter with a Lesson. Ms. Small is a motivational speaker, trainer, and humor consultant.

Again, thank you so much. I've really enjoyed it.

Small

Thank you. It's been a real honor and a complete pleasure.

About the Author

Carol Ann Small, founder of Laughter with a Lesson, works with organizations that want to boost morale, reduce stress, and create a happy workforce. Ms. Small's customized, humorous keynotes and seminars have entertained and educated employees for over a decade. Her name may be "Small," but her vibrant presence is larger than life.

Carol Ann Small
Laughter with a Lesson
(781) 662-2078 or (888) 393-6926
E-mail: CarolAnn@SmallSpeak.com
www.CarolAnnSmall.com

Chapter Three – Bruce Jenner

-

David Wright (Wright)

Today we're talking to Bruce Jenner. Bruce captivated the world when he broke the world record by scoring 8,634 points in the decathlon at the 1976 Olympic games in Montreal and earned the title World's Greatest Athlete. In the years following his athletic achievements, Mr. Jenner has become a successful and highly respected motivational speaker, sports commentator, entrepreneur, commercial spokesperson, television personality, actor, producer, and author. Mr. Jenner serves on numerous advisory boards, such as the Special Olympics. He also serves on the Council of Champions and the National Dyslexia Research Foundation. He is an avid supporter of Athletes and Entertainers for Kids. Mr. Jenner and his wife, Kris, serve on the board of the Dream Foundation, an organization that grants wishes to terminally ill adults. He has been a guest on *Oprah, The Tonight Show with Jay Leno,* and *Regis and Kathie Lee.* He is a highly regarded and successful author. His newest release is *Finding the Champion Within.*

Bruce Jenner, welcome to *Mission Possible!*

Bruce Jenner (Jenner)

It's my pleasure; but you know that title, World's Greatest Athlete? It doesn't help my golf game!

Wright

I hear you're a ten handicap.

Jenner

Actually, I'm about a three or four right now. I've worked pretty hard on it; but when you're standing over that six-foot putt with six inches of break, titles don't seem to help—it keeps you pretty humble.

Wright

With all these titles—actor, athlete, spokesman, author—I read that you've been named Father of the Year by the U.S. Jaycees, and received the Father of the Year honors from the Southern California Father's Day Committee. Those are impressive honors.

Jenner

That's just because I have ten children. If you have ten children and you're still standing, boom! you get an immediate Father of the Year award. I've been very blessed in that department—six girls and four boys, ages twenty-three to four. I do the father thing every day, and I'm very lucky.

Wright

Those are great honors for a person whose time has been in such demand for years. Has family always been a number one priority for you?

Jenner

Definitely, especially in my type of business where you're out in the public. You get very plastic, very "surfacy." But your real life is with your family. That real life—taking the garbage out, carpools, relationships, good days, bad days, and on and on and on—is by far what I live with my family and the everyday stuff that I do. Then I get out there and motivate people and try to build some businesses.

Wright

While preparing for this interview, I got the feeling that a commitment to youth has always been important to you, especially the physically and mentally challenged. Is this a response to your own battle with dyslexia?

Jenner

Yes, because I can really identify with these kids. To be honest with you, being dyslexic myself, I always tell kids that if you're dyslexic and that's the only problem you have in life, you've got it made. You can deal with this thing. The bigger problem than being dyslexic is a lack of self-confidence in yourself, especially at a young age. When you're growing up and everybody's accelerating in school and doing well, and reading seems to be simple for everybody else, but for you perceptually picking those words up off the piece of paper is tough, you lose confidence in yourself. In my case, that's basically what I did. I lost interest in school; I flunked second grade; I didn't want to go to school. My biggest fear in life was to go to school, because I was afraid the teacher was going to make me read in front of the class. Not only perceptually did I have a hard time getting the words off the piece of paper, but also I got so emotionally upset because I didn't want to look bad in front of my friends. It just didn't work.

But it molded me into the type of person I am today. I always tell kids if I had not been dyslexic I would not have won the games, because being dyslexic made me special, made me different from everyone else. When I found what I call my little arena to play in, which happened to be sports, it became very important to me. I excelled at that. Not that later on down the line, after years and years of doing this, I always thought about the dyslexic thing, but that little dyslexic kid was always sitting in the back of my head outworking the next guy. I look at athletics in two ways: the athletic body and the athletic mind. I was given okay athletic skills physically; but being a kid who grew up with a lack of self-confidence, I found out my greatest gift was my athletic brain. I could outperform people under pressure because my brain worked so well, and I could come up with the performances when everyone else was dying. Dealing with pressure and fear and all those types of things you have to deal with, I was better at than anybody else. So it was an interesting metamorphosis through life.

Wright

Did anyone in your early years ever call you dumb or stupid?

Jenner

No, but I always felt dumb and stupid, because I was always in the slower classes in grade school growing up. Nobody had to say anything. It was more my own internal struggles that I was dealing with.

Wright

I talked to a good friend of yours, Billy Blades, the other day, and I also talked to Les Brown, who is a tremendous motivational speaker in the country. Both of these men told me the same story. They were dyslexic, and it almost devastated their childhood; they didn't find out about it until they were thirty-seven.

Jenner

I remember in junior high school one day they gave it a name and said, "You're dyslexic." I wondered if that was bad, if I was going to die from this. It was a pretty bad word. They said, "No, go back to class. Have a good day." That was about the extent of it back then. Actually, for a while it became too big a word. If any kid wrote anything backwards, they were dyslexic. It became a catch phrase for a lot of different problems. It's calmed down a little bit now. They've been able to analyze things like this. It's not the end of the world if you're dyslexic.

Remember the movie *City Slickers,* with Curly and Billy Crystal sitting by the fire? Billy Crystal asks Curly, the old wise cowboy, "What's the secret to life?" He says, "One thing," and the conversation continues. Finally, later on in the conversation, Billy Crystal asks, "What's that one thing?" Curly looks over and says, "That's for you to find out." That's so true. In life I was lucky at a young age to find this thing called sports. I found that I had an aptitude for that. That brought me out of my shell and helped me feel good about myself, which helped the self-confidence problems. The challenge for young kids today who are suffering with something like this is to find their niche in life. That's a parent's responsibility. It doesn't have to be in sports. It could be in a million different fields. Tom Cruise is dyslexic, and Cher—the list goes on and on and on of people who found their niche. I try to encourage kids to go out there and try art, try music, try acting; who knows where is your talent? If it's taken away in one area, it's given to you in another. Your job is to find the other area and then go with it.

Wright

You have a new motivational book out titled *Finding the Champion Within,* published by Simon and Schuster. Tell us a little about it and who will benefit from reading it.

Jenner

I think everybody will. The reason I call it *Finding the Champion Within* is that when I was growing up, I never knew down deep in my soul if I had anything special down there. But every time I'd dig down deeper and deeper through athletics, which was testing me in competition all the time, I realized that there was something there, and I didn't even know what it was. Going through that long process and going through the games and being able to win and stand on top of the platform and all that—probably the one thing that gave me is confidence in people. We all have that champion that lives down deep inside that has the ability to overcome tremendous obstacles in our life and to do tremendous things with our life. But there's a process to finding that. With the book and through my speaking I talk about that process and try to motivate people to basically believe in themselves.

That's why I did the book. The speaking is kind of tough, because I run all over the United States to primarily sales forces, but also to all kinds of groups, and talk about finding the champion within. The travel's tough and I'm away from home and all of that, but I really enjoy the presentation. It took that performance in 1976 and that great journey that I was on, and it didn't die back then. It still lives on to help motivate people and to move people forward in their lives. It may be one line, one sentence, one word within that might spark one person to say, "Hey, I do believe in myself, and I can do these things."

Wright

I remember reading a program that was produced by a company in Waco, Texas, called Success Motivation Institute, with a fellow named Paul Meyer. He did a program called "The Making of a Champion," and you were featured in one of the stories. It was very motivational. Wheaties has just commemorated its seventy-fifth anniversary, and you're back on the front of the box along with other superstar athletes like Tiger Woods and Michael Jordan. How does that feel after earning the title World's Greatest Athlete twenty-six years ago?

Jenner

To be honest with you, it's very flattering, mostly because when I got out of the games I went into the television world, the commercial world, and all the types of things I've been doing over the past years. It's very nice and very flattering to be in the top fifty athletes of the past decade and things like that. It's nice to have in my memory bank. I don't live on it or dwell on it in my own personal life, but it certainly is a nice position to be in. Obviously, I was very proud of that day, and it was a great day. I had trained for twelve years of my life for that moment, and I came through. I'm proud of that. It's a nice, very positive message—sometimes in our world today we need positive messages.

Wright

You're a highly respected motivational speaker today. What is the message that corporations want and need to hear in today's economy?

Jenner

You have to have a belief system. Two years ago we were riding high. Everything was just wonderful; everyone was making money; the stock market was going through the roof, on and on. Today we need to look at things probably more realistically than we did back then. We kind of had our heads in the sky. Today we have to be a lot more realistic; we can't just wander through life. Especially with 9/11 and all the things that we're going through in our country, we have to take life seriously. You get this great shot. You get seventy-five years, on average, that you're on this planet, and you've got to go for it. I always feel like everybody is at their best when they wake up in the morning and they're excited about that day, whether it's building a business, improving their relationship with their family, whatever it may be. When you get up in the morning, you've got to be excited about tackling that day, one day at a time. You constantly build on these days, day after day after day, and eventually you've really accomplished something. You've moved forward in your life. You've overcome a lot of things. Today you've got to be smart in what you're doing.

Wright

Did 9/11 have any impact specifically on your life or the life of your family?

Jenner

I think probably everybody knows somebody who was in those buildings and lost their life. We have one friend whose husband was in the building. She was eight months pregnant and daddy never came home. A month later she had the baby; she's a very close friend of ours. I think everybody is affected. You'd have to be a cold, heartless person to be sitting there watching on the 11th of September and not be affected. I was stuck in a hotel room in Milwaukee, sitting there all day long watching everything that was going on and was just devastated by it.

The world changed that day. Our attitudes changed that day. It was a terrible, terrible tragedy, but I will say one thing—it certainly has brought our country together. It certainly has shown the world that we are not going to tolerate those types of things. You attack us and you've got big problems. We've shown a very strong hand, and I think our country is dealing with it very well. There's nothing wrong with a little bit of patriotism out there. We have the greatest country in the world, and I'm proud to be part of it.

Wright

When you're standing up there with the gold medal hanging around your neck and the band is playing our national anthem and the flag is going up, does that really have an impact on the rest of your life?

Jenner

It does have an impact on the rest of your life in the sense that forever you'll always be an Olympic champion. It's a pretty elite fraternity out there. That's the main thing that it does. When I went into the games I was the favorite; I was the world record holder. It was the last meet of my life. It was the last time I was ever going to do these things. But when I walked away I had accomplished everything in a sport I wanted to accomplish. I broke the world record three times, I had the Olympic record, I had the gold medal, number one in the world for three years. I walked away smiling because I was so happy that I could walk away accomplishing everything that I wanted to accomplish. Very few athletes can do that, walk away saying they did everything in the sport they could possibly do. It was a great career, and now I'm moving on.

In my sport there is no longevity. I don't go to my friends and say, "Are we going to go throw the shot or pole vault today?" No, we're going to go play golf. It wasn't like Tiger Woods, after he won the Masters, throwing his golf clubs away and never touching a golf club the rest of his life. I had to do that. I had to walk away from my best friend. But I knew that, and I knew that going in. Was it hard? Yes, it was hard. I was the best in the world at what I did. It's kind of like a piano player, who for twelve years of his life sits in front of that piano banging out that music. You get your chance, you go in front of the rest of the world, you play the most beautiful music the world's ever heard, and when the song's over, you put your hands in your pockets and you never touch the piano again.

That was kind of sad from my stance. It was a bittersweet kind of moment. It was great and satisfying to win, but I was also sad I was leaving my best friend. It was kind of an interesting thing to go through. I realized the reason I was walking away. Roger Bannister had a quote about sports and life; he said, "Only in something like running can finality be achieved, but it is not the type of finality that leaves you with nothing to live for, because sport is not the main aim in life. Yet to achieve perfection in one area, however small, makes it possible to face uncertainties in the more difficult problems in life." That's a great quote. That's what sports is all about: go in there, compete hard, and then move on in life to the more important things.

Wright

I'm old enough to remember Roger Bannister.

Jenner

He was the first man to break four minutes in the mile.

Wright

Some of the greatest athletes in the world have taken up golf. Michael Jordan is an example. He would rather play golf than basketball. Why is that?

Jenner

It's just a very challenging game. I play on what's called a Celebrity Players Tour. I played one event this weekend up in Las Vegas. There were about eighty guys. They call it the Celebrity Players Tour, but it's probably ninety-five percent retired athletes. It's just a great game. Even when you get a little older, you still enjoy the competition, the competitive spirit, the camaraderie with all the other guys that are out there. It's a difficult and frustrating game. It looks so simple, but it's so difficult to do. It's a great challenge. It's a totally different pace than what you're used to. In my days of competing, I was in the Olympic arena. I was out there grunting and groaning in training. Golf's just the opposite. You're out there with your friends; you're enjoying the game; it's a beautiful day. You're on a golf course—a highly competitive, difficult sport, and it makes it fun. You can do it the rest of your life. It's not like you have to give it up in a few years because your knees go. In most cases, you can do it until you're seventy.

Wright

My brother was a golf instructor and he took me out. I was a weekend duffer and couldn't play at all. I just went for the fun. He got me out one day with nothing but a nine iron and knocked twenty-five strokes off my game. He told me to throw the rest of them away and just keep that one.

Jenner

He was smart; he knew what he was doing.

Wright

With our *Mission Possible!* talk show and book, we are trying to encourage people in our audience to be better, live better, and be more fulfilled by listening to the examples of our guests. Is there anyone or anything in your life that has made a difference for you and helped you become a better person?

Jenner

You have to pick the number one person in your life, and that's my wife, Kris. We've been very blessed with a lot of children. We've been married a long time now. That's your soul mate, the person you spend every day with. That's who you talk with about everything. So number one would be my wife. We're very fortunate and have been blessed in a lot of ways. By far, my wife. She's been the best—my bud!

Wright

She works with you now, doesn't she?

Jenner

Yes, she runs the offices. She keeps me organized—too organized, I think!

Wright

I was reading about an old track coach of yours, L.D. Weldon, who is credited with having been the first person to really recognize the great potential that you obviously showed later on. Was he a mentor of sorts?

Jenner

To be honest, I'd almost have to consider L.D. as my second dad. I lived in his home in college. He asked me to come out to this little dinky school in Iowa in the late sixties. When you're eighteen to twenty-two, there are a lot of things going on in your life. He was a great human being to be around. He was a great person with good moral standing, good guidance, just a great person to be around. He was a character. L.D. always liked multi-eventers, and he actually had recruited me to play football. I lasted about three weeks and had to have knee surgery, so that was a short career. Fortunately, it was the best injury I ever had, because it got me out of that sport. He was not the technical coach that just sat there and worked on technique; he was a motivator. He'd help you out with as much technique as I think he was possible of doing, but he was such a great guy and such a great motivator that you didn't want to lose races because you didn't want to let L.D. down. He's had great decathlon guys in the past. He was sixty-five when we met, and he'd had a guy in the 1936 Olympic games. His name was Jack Parker, and he took the bronze medal in Berlin.

To be honest with you, my favorite picture that I have is a picture of L.D. standing there with his fist clenched and he's got his hat on. He always used to brag about every athlete he ever had. We had to listen to every story about every athlete, but he signed this picture, "To Bruce, the greatest athlete I ever coached. L.D. Weldon." To me, knowing L.D. was a really, really big deal. That was very special. He was a great human being and great for those years from eighteen to twenty-two for guidance and that type of thing.

Wright

I remember as a kid seeing Burt Lancaster play Jim Thorpe, the all-American. I jumped every hedge on the way home from the theater. It motivated me.

Jenner

Oh, yeah, I remember that. They did Jim Thorpe. They did Bob Mathias, a story on his life. When I started running the decathlon—1970 was my first one—I didn't even think about the Olympics. The reason I got so excited about it is that the guys in the past who had won the Olympic decathlon were not just Olympic champions, they almost became part of American history. Jim Thorpe, Bob Mathias, Rafer Johnson—these guys were bigger than life, because it was such a tough event. That was one of the motivating factors. To be honest with you, as I got closer and closer to the games, I didn't care what happened. I just wanted to stand on the same stage as a Rafer Johnson, Toomey, Mathias, or all these guys in the past who had won it. It's a tough deal to win.

Wright

After seeing the movie, I read the life story of Bob Matthias. I just couldn't believe it. Have you ever met him?

Jenner

He's a great friend and a great human being.

Wright

What do you think makes up a great mentor? In other words, are there characteristics that mentors seem to have in common?

Jenner

Yes. First of all they have to be giving people. A mentor has to be, I think, of great moral character. I think that's extremely important. It's like what is called the MasterMind Principle. You find out what you do and what you want to become in life, and you go and associate with those people that are doing it. That's extremely strong; having somebody in your life who has been through experiences, who is willing to help you, is extremely important. You are a lot of what your surroundings are. It's important to find those people out and associate yourself with those types of people, from your family, your parents, the kids you hang out with, the other adults you hang out with. Things like that, growing up, are extremely important. Who are the people that you're looking up to? That's important in life.

Wright

You've influenced so many people around you. I've talked to your daughter a few times. Does she work in your company?

Jenner

Yes, four years of paying for college and she works for us! She started for us four years ago, but she's looking at other options now, so I don't know how long she'll hang out with us.

Wright

Most people are fascinated with the new TV shows about being a survivor. What has been the greatest comeback you have made from adversity in your career or life?

Jenner

Overcoming the dyslexic problem would probably be it. The old saying, "Success is not measured by heights attained, but by obstacles overcome." Little things like, for me, my biggest fear was going to school because I was afraid the teacher was going to make me read in front of the class. I hated that. I sat there with sweaty palms all day long in fear that it was going to happen. Cut to years later. I go to the games, I win the games, I get a job. It's one of the first things they have you do—teleprompter work. I panic. That little dyslexic kid is there. But I was able to go out there and find my own ways to get around it, to be able to do those kinds of things. I used to host *Good Morning America* when David Hartman or one of the others was gone. That was two hours of teleprompter reading, on and on. For me, I overcame more to do that than I did to win the games.

Little things like that along the way. I have to say I really lost interest in a lot of things in the middle eighties. Then I met my wife. We got married eleven years ago, and being with somebody you love gives you more reason to work. It's not just about working for yourself. I didn't care that much about it; I hadn't worked for years. But finding somebody and renewing the family, adding more kids on to the family, starts to kick you in the butt. I had to start getting serious about life again. It's not just about little old me, because I don't need that much. But now I've got a family and a four-year-old and a six-year-old. It motivates you to get back out there and get some things going.

Wright

When you consider the choices you have made down through the years, has faith played an important role in your life?

Jenner

To a point. I believe in God and go to church, not regularly, but I go. I believe God gave me a life, gave me some talents, to do with what I can. And then the rest is up to me. My success or failure is going to be determined by myself. I take personal responsibility for my life, and I've always felt that. I've always felt like I had Godgiven talents, good points and bad points. My job is to use those things, to get out there and make something of myself. To wake up in the morning and feel good about myself is my responsibility. I can't say, "Oh, I failed and it was God's will." No, I failed and it was my problem. Or, "I was successful, and it was in the glory of God." I always feel like I worked hard. God gave me some talent, and I'm the one who worked hard, and if He's looking down on me and saying, "You did a good job," that's all I need.

Wright
In reading about you, I was interested in the Longevity Network. Are you still involved in that?

Jenner
Yes, we're a network marketing company based in Henderson, Nevada. We sell all kinds of products. We've been doing this for eight or nine years.

Wright
Is it all health related?

Jenner
We do health-related stuff; we do hair care products, all kinds of stuff for home-based business entrepreneurs. We have vitamin programs, weight loss programs, all sorts of stuff.

Wright
I interviewed Dr. Mendel the other day, and he was talking about the health revolution. It was like a war to him. He said each year about 140,000 Americans die from adverse effects from prescription drugs, and almost one million are injured due to dispensing errors. He said people are going to have to take control of their own life and their own health in terms of vitamins, running, exercising, and those sorts of things.

Jenner
I certainly agree with that. We have to take responsibility, and again it comes down to it's our responsibility to take care of our health and eat properly. Honestly, it's not that difficult. It just has to be a priority. Sometimes we don't take our health seriously until something goes wrong. Then it's the wake-up call. Eating properly, to me, is the 80/20 Theory. Eighty percent of the time you eat what normally you would think of as good food; the other twenty percent, have fun. Have a little Häagen-Dazs, a little of this and that; you can have a little fun with those things. But eighty percent of the time you have to eat right. Then you can kind of splurge and have a good time.

Exercise is interesting. The CDC came out with a study back in '96, I think it was, basically saying that living a sedentary lifestyle is as hazardous to your health as if you smoke. That's pretty scary, but that's the bad news. The good news was that a moderate amount of exercise, just a little bit of exercise, has as positive effect on your health as if you're a marathoner. So the good news here is that a little bit goes a long ways. That's an important study. A lot of the reason people don't exercise is that if they're living a relatively sedentary lifestyle, they think doing exercise is like running the 10K, because that's what they see people doing. They say, "I could never do that." But can they walk up three flights of stairs instead of taking the elevator? You certainly can do that. Just doing a little and realizing that you don't have to run marathons or go to the gym five times a week—you just have to live an active lifestyle. Get as much exercise in your daily life as you can. If you're in an apartment, or your office is on the fifth floor, don't take the elevator—walk up. Everybody always looks for the closest parking place for the grocery store. Find one that's far away and walk. There are a lot of ways just to get some activity in your life, which is going to have a very positive effect on your health.

Wright

Speaking of health, I remember reading about something you had created called Personal Blood Storage, Inc. What is that all about?

Jenner

Back in the late eighties, early nineties a friend came to me and said he was starting a business called Personal Blood Storage. Basically, what he had developed was the technology to store blood at 70° C below zero. They had been able to freeze blood, because it's an individual cell freezing process instead of like an organ, which if you try to freeze is cell on cell, and it breaks itself up and doesn't work very well, at least not yet—they'll probably figure it out someday. But they've been freezing blood for years. The problem was they didn't have freezer capacity; they only had small freezers. So he developed this technology, and he was going to do personal blood storage. It was a very interesting entrepreneurial effort. The concept was so much better than the blood banks that are out there now. In each freezer we could do about 45,000 units of blood. The blood system in the United States doesn't freeze. The Red Cross is a monopoly, and they don't freeze blood, so every thirty days they have to turn over the blood supply. That's why they're constantly asking for blood. I can tell you right now, the first two weeks of January the Red Cross will be on the news saying that they need blood because for the last month, because of the holidays, nobody's been giving blood, so the system is out and there's no reserve. Personal Blood Storage would allow you to put your own blood away if you wanted to. Over a year's period you could put four or five pints of blood away, store it, and if you ever needed it, it would be there so you would have your own blood. Or you could start to build up a reservoir, a supply of blood that's on the side, so in case of a tragedy you would always have blood available. Well, the Red Cross is a monopoly. The poor guy spent a lot of money and got shut down every place he went. It was ruthless. The Red Cross came after us because they didn't want the competition. So after about five years of spending a lot of money and trying to fight the Red Cross in every trench, he finally said he'd had enough.

Wright

The reason I was so interested in it is that just last week someone was telling me that if I ever needed any kind of surgery and had some time before I had the surgery, to always go in and donate my own blood so there would be no rejection. Is that the basic principle?

Jenner

Yes, it's your blood. Why would you want to put somebody else's blood in you if you could use your own blood? The concept for it is fabulous, except you're going up against a monopoly.

Wright

It's encouraging that you still go mountain biking, run on the track at Pepperdine, play golf, are a commercially rated pilot, and race cars professionally in the Grand Prix events. That's pretty cool.

Jenner

I live a very active life and I enjoy doing a lot of things. That's why I was a decathlon guy.

Wright

If you could have a platform and tell our audience something you feel would help or encourage them, what would you say?

Jenner

Four words, which are the keys to success in life: gamble, cheat, lie, and steal! *Gamble*—gamble your best shot in life. Dare to take risks. Life has got to be a great adventure or it's nothing. *Cheat*—cheat those who would have you be less than you are. Surround yourself with positive people, uplifting people, people who want to see you do well. Turn around and help them and you're truly a champion. *Lie*—lie in the arms of those that you love. When it comes right down to it, all we have is one another. Never take the love that you give or the love that you receive for granted. Finally, *steal*—steal everyone with happiness. Live every day as if it's your last, because we never know when that day is going to come. Gamble, cheat, lie, and steal.

Wright

That's great advice from a great American.

We have been talking today to Bruce Jenner, who literally captivated us all when he broke the world record in 1976 in the Olympic Games, and he's still at it, as we have just found out. He's not only an athlete but a great business person and a much requested speaker.

Mr. Jenner, we really appreciate you being with us today on *Mission Possible!* It's been a personal privilege for me.

Jenner

It was a lot of fun. It was great having a chance to talk to you.

About the Author

After winning a gold medal in the 1976 Olympic Games, Bruce Jenner has gone on to winning seasons in life. He's known to millions as a motivational speaker, TV personality, sports commentator, commercial spokesperson, entrepreneur, actor and producer.

Bruce Jenner
www.brucejenner.com

Chapter Four – Dr. Bonnie Libhart

-

David E. Wright (Wright)

Today we are talking to Bonnie Libhart, former CEO for an international manufacturing corporation, a unique professional speaker, trainer, consultant, and author of several books. Bonnie has interviewed over five thousand people as host of ABC's *Scene Today.* She began her career hosting radio and TV talk shows in North Carolina, Pennsylvania, Ohio, Tennessee, Arkansas, and Texas. As a producer of her own talk show in Waco, Texas, Bonnie won the coveted Abe Lincoln Award for excellence in broadcasting.

Bonnie Libhart, welcome to *Mission Possible!*

Bonnie Libhart (Libhart)

Well, thank you very much, David Wright.

Wright

Bonnie, I was interested in the topics that you use in your speaking and training, specifically humor in business and stress management. Are the two topics related?

Libhart

Absolutely, David. There was a study done by a University of Arkansas research team that determined if you have humor, you can communicate more effectively and the person will accept more of what you're trying to communicate. Sometimes you can be stressed to the max, and adding a little humor will dissipate some of the stress.

There are three major secrets to the art of communication and how stress and humor are interrelated. If you can add humor to a stressful situation, there will be more clarity. If you work with a company and sometimes the employees in the organization feel that there's too much stress, you can add a little levity and have so much fun at work that it will help everyone involved.

I said there were three primary secrets, as far as I'm concerned, and I call them FUN. FUN is an acronym. If you have ever been a smoker and dropped a big ole red ash on your sleeve, you wouldn't just let it burn through your jacket or your arm; you would flick it off. That's what I think the F stands for. When you're in a stressful situation, just *flick off* what people say by mentally thinking that they could be stressed themselves. Perhaps they're trying to say something negative to you. If you don't take it so seriously, it will help the entire situation, and humor is one of the ways that can be done. The U in what I call the three secrets is to *unglue*. What I mean by unglue is just set yourself apart so that you don't feel so "into" the situation. There was a great man in one of the best sellers that has ever been, the Good Book, the Bible, where the Apostle Paul said, "Put those things behind which are behind." Even if it's in the moment, in your opinion, think of something that will unglue yourself from the situation. In that way, you will feel that there is hope with what's going on. The N, or third secret, is to do what you have to do *now*.

If you can create a little humor in a stressful situation, then you can really create an environment that will not only motivate yourself but will motivate others. It simply inspires everyone to be a team, whether it's in the home or in business. I think that laughter gives you the edge, because you could have a know-it-all boss or a co-worker who is a control freak (which I have been accused of being in my lifetime), and you can actually get that person on your side with a little humor. A little levity also provides a good attitude so that if you do not have all the "book learning" that you need (as they say out in the plant, Welding 101 is not taught at Harvard), you can get people to laugh with you and not at you. You can take a disaster and turn it into a positive. I believe that stress can be dissipated with some levity, humor, and laughter.

Wright

Well, that's easy to remember: *flick, unglue,* and *now*.

Bonnie, having known you for many years, I believe your presentation on family and personal development is a topic that is very close to your heart. Can you tell us why?

Libhart

One of the reasons that I feel that family and personal development are so close to my heart is that when we meet someone and marry them, or when we deal with our parents, peers, or other people in our lives, we tend to look at their actions through rose-colored glasses. Then reality sets in, and we find that when we feel that things that go wrong are someone else's fault, we discover a beam in our own eye.

For example, my daughter spoke Russian, and as a part of her job she took people to the former Soviet Union on missionary trips. On one of her trips she was killed, and all that followed had a damaging effect on our family. I could see how the event was destroying our family, and I knew that the healing process would be in direct proportion to how I handled the loss. I've been working with Dr. Phil McGraw's group called Pathways in Dallas. He's the man that's on *Oprah* every week and has a program helping people resolve their personal conflicts. Most of the time the solutions are within us. It's not so much what David Wright does to Mrs. David Wright, or Tony Libhart does to Bonnie; it's our reaction to what happens. When my daughter got killed, my son and another daughter felt angry with her, because they felt she had left them. She had told me as a young woman, "Don't worry, Mother; when you get older, I'll take care of you." So I had a little resentment. I thought, The one who was going to take care of me got killed! I found that if we don't learn to handle our own stress and our own family's personal development, we're not winning in the game of life.

Wright

Bonnie, I remember reading a story that you shared a few years ago about the sixty-second running of the Indy 500. Could you tell us a little bit about it?

Libhart

I was working for ABC television at the time. It was really exciting, because I was one of the first women to get a pass to be in the pit area. An Indy 500 pace car came streaking straight toward me and my husband, Tony. There were about fifty fellow journalists on a flimsy press stand in the pit area of the Indianapolis Motor Speedway. I remember thinking, "Hey, the pace car has lost control. It's going too fast. It's going to hit!" It was just seconds before the open convertible carrying former astronaut John Glenn and three other race officials screamed off the track, skidded over the apron, and, before any of us could do anything or realize the horrific scene that was coming, the inevitable crash, the car slammed into the safety fence and into our bleachers.

A souvenir hunter had stolen the flag that normally waves the drivers where they should start braking, so it was just one of those things. I saw around me splintered two-by-fours from the handrails of the temporary stands. It all just rained down, and I saw human figures.

It was almost as if I were watching a movie, because I thought that it couldn't be happening to me. Human figures were bouncing and ricocheting from the steps. It was like when my mother used to put water in a hot iron skillet, and I'd see that water jump up and down.

Seeing the pictures, I don't really remember this; but somebody had a video camera going, and I somersaulted into the air and landed on the pace car. Actually, Tony landed on the hood, and I did get to sit in John Glenn's lap for a few seconds. I thought it was going to be my death. I was in shock and just started moving. It was as if in slow motion, and I automatically started to grope for our belongings while looking for Tony. I raised my head and saw men pulling my husband from the steaming hood of the pace car. His white jeans and his shirt that had Indy 500 on it were spattered with blood. Still dazed, I crawled to Tony's side. He was unconscious, but my mind was fully awakened. Though my body was bruised, it was my swarming thoughts that hurt and stung: O God, help me! I brought Tony here to keep him quiet, to forward my career; did I bring him here to die? There were several people who were really hurt—I think there were twenty-four from all over the world.

At the time, I worked at ABC television in Jonesboro, Arkansas, and the sports director couldn't go, so that's how Tony ended up at the race. Tony had been very resentful of the frequent trips I would take away from our home and three children. Since he was a photographer for his company and a design engineer professionally, he was really first-rate with a camera. As a boy, he always dreamed of going to the Indy 500. We successfully covered other news events for the TV station, but in the recent years our marriage partnership had developed all the marks of failure. We both earned good money, and I saw to it that we lived to the limit of our two incomes. We had a Mercedes back in those days and wardrobes with white mink coats. There were always those nagging feelings inside of me—accusations, sarcasm, self-justification, and he would yell at me or say to me, "You ought to spend more time with the kids, Bonnie." I would say to him, "You ought to help more around the house." Well, I couldn't be a mother and also compare him favorably to the aggressive and flashy men that were at the TV station.

I had grown up poor, in the typical Arkansas cotton patch with no electricity or indoor plumbing. My kids kept saying, "Yes, we know. It was three miles walking barefoot in the snow; now it's ten miles." With my background of rural poverty, I had a strong incentive to achieve, and I was proud to be a local celebrity and to be on television.

I used my own fat paycheck—it was *his* money, *my* money, and *our* money. I wanted to buy all the things that money could buy, and I was blind to spending and blind to my love for Tony. He lay there after the accident with one eye hanging down. Later, I wondered where they had taken him when they left in a helicopter to get him to a hospital in Indianapolis. And while I was sitting there in the room waiting and wondering, with my life just going before me, I thought, Will he make it? If only I could let him know how much I really do care about him.

When the helicopter took him away, there was not enough room for me, so I had to go find the car through 200,050 other cars. Back in those days, I wore false eyelashes (I called them the Tammy Baker eyelashes), and because I had been crying, wondering if he was going to make it, one eyelash was slip sliding down my face. I looked around at all the other people, and it looked as if they were having a normal day. I thought, How can people feel so normal when I'm going through this trauma, wondering if he's going to live? Why hadn't I been able to see the value of our family and our marriage prior to that? The doctor came down within the next twenty-four hours and told me they were able to sew his eye back in place. They had put a platinum plate in his head, and he was going to be okay. They tested his eyesight and he could see. I was so appreciative.

After that, there were major changes in me. I turned money matters over to Tony, because he's really much better at financial management than I. I actually had a hidden benefit. I don't know whether or not this has happened to other people who've gone through traumatic experiences, but I had a new respect for Tony's wisdom and ability. And even though it's been a few years since the Indy 500 pace car struck us, I've recognized that God used the shock of a sudden, life-threatening accident to help us revive and revitalize a dying marriage.

Wright
Something must have happened.

Libhart
I tell you, I found a prayer to claim. It was in Psalm 119:37, which says to turn my eyes from looking at vanities and "give me life in thy way."

Wright

While preparing for this interview, I read that you and your husband, Tony, had a born-again marriage. What does that mean? Does that have something to do with what you're talking about?

Libhart

Yes, absolutely. We had been church members, church goers, and, in fact, even taught a Sunday school class. Because he didn't know my situation—I only had a concussion; fortunately, my old hard head kept me from getting any serious injury—there was such a new love and respect for each other . . . what I call a born-again marriage. It's as if you fall in love all over again. You start admiring and respecting the other partner in your life and get your eyes off your own selfish ways. I was able to see him though eyes that weren't clouded with my own selfish desires.

Wright

Over twenty years ago I worked with you and a few other people in Waco, Texas. I remember you were working there to establish goal setting in the fabric of my company. I know you're an advocate as well as a teacher of goal setting. Could you tell us why it makes such a difference in the lives of people?

Libhart

Goal setting is so incredibly successful for my family and me and for the people I teach. I was just looking at some of the goals I had written out. I call them smart goals, and I like to use an acronym to remember them: S being *specific*, M being *measurable*, A being *attainable*, R being *realistic*, and T is that they have to be *time sensitive.* I was looking back at some of the things that I've written down. One was a loan that we owed. I wanted, by a certain date, to have it paid off. Another was to add some carpet to the house. Also, I wanted to start my book. I always set a deadline when I have an idea.

You might remember that John Grisham wrote a book called *The Painted House.* He lived only fifteen or twenty miles from my house in Arkansas, and when I read *The Painted House,* I realized it could have been my autobiography. In rural Arkansas he had overcome several adversities too. We all go through a lot of adversities, whether it's the loss of a child or bankruptcy, which we experienced when we started our own company and ended up paying back a large amount of money. It took us ten years to pay back 1.4 million dollars that we owed people from starting our company. We sold the product line to another company and were able to pay people back over a period of time. The only reason we could do it was because of our written goals.

Whether it's my own children, my grandchildren, or those people I teach in my classes, I really impress upon people to put a date by their goals. I make so many resolutions, as many of us do, around the holidays, and what I have found is that if you make those resolutions realistic, they will be easier to keep. Whatever your goal is, just look at the end results. I love the saying, "Call into being those things which are not, as if they were." Remember, it's paper. If we don't reach the goal at that moment, we can set another date. I heard this from a senator: "Fill your mouth with marbles when you set a goal, and every time you reach a goal, take out a marble. You will know you've reached all of your goals when you have lost all your marbles."

Wright

Great saying!

Bonnie, with our *Mission Possible!* talk show and book, we're trying to encourage people in our audience to live better, be better, and be more fulfilled by listening to the examples of our guests. Is there anyone or anything in your life that has made a difference for you and helped you to become a better person?

Libhart

Absolutely. I would have to start with my mother. She had the most influence. She was a formal schoolteacher, but she didn't teach when the five of us were born and growing up. My mom had all these sayings that continue to go through my mind day after day: "If a task is once begun, do not leave it till it's done; be it labor great or small, do it well or not at all." She also taught me to inspect what you expect.

I think Dr. Phil McGraw has been an influence in my life. With his Pathways program, he helped me identify where I came from, where I am now, and where I want to go in the future. Also, Paul J. Meyer has helped me. I would not give anything for what Success Motivation Institute has meant to me. Zig Ziglar has been a great influence on my life through the National Speakers Association. When he found out my daughter was killed, he wrote a personal letter to me. That tells me a lot about him. My dad had influence as well. He simply believed in me and loved me so much—not that he ever told me he loved me, and not that he ever hugged me, but I knew my daddy believed in me.

Wright

When you consider the choices that you have made down through the years, has faith played an important roll in your life?

Libhart

David, faith has been my anchor when all around appeared to be falling apart. In the last twelve months, we've had seven family members pass on to heaven, including my mom, one of my brothers, and three of my husband's brothers. I found that if you're anchored in faith way down inside of you, you know that all things work together for good, that you are doing the very best that you can, and the decisions you make today are the best you can make with the knowledge and the circumstances and the environment that you're in. Faith has always shown me that we can make it, because we do have the mind of Christ. In the Old Testament, Psalm 84:11 says that the Lord is a sun and shield. Now, the sun lights our way and the shield protects us from all the dangers. And He will give grace and glory. Grace is unmerited favor, and we have the favor just because we are children of God, created in His image. We want to have favor with all the people we're with. And glory—that doesn't mean we glory in ourselves, but He glories in us being created in His image. It's as if no good thing shall be withheld from David Wright, who walks uprightly. That has been one of my loved anchors. I believe we are guided and directed and that we get back what we feed out.

I work with Jeannie C. Riley a lot, and one of her songs talks about casting our bread upon the water. You notice when a pebble is dropped in a stream, the little waves from it ripple all the way over to the bank and beyond, to a lake or wherever you are, and that's the way our lives are. We touch the next person, who touches the next person.

We were in Philadelphia on September 11, when they told us to get out of town. We had toured and seen the Liberty Bell the night before, and so we went up to Nazareth, Pennsylvania, where some friends of ours were living at the time. We saw this horrendous thing that happened to our country, but they didn't achieve their goal of bringing you and me down, because we have faith. We have an anchor within us and a belief in us and in our God and in our country and in the basic goodness of humankind.

Wright

If you could have a platform and tell our audience something that you feel would help or encourage them, what would you say to them?

Libhart

Get up one more time! Each of us has been placed here on earth and given life for one good purpose. Each of us has been given a gift. It was put in us to develop, and through the development, we bless humanity. That is the ordained purpose behind each of our lives. Your purpose can only be accomplished by you. You can be you better than anyone else can be you. In fact, I have a premonition about you, David. I have this premonition that soars on silver wings. I know of your accomplishments with all the books and things you've done and other wondrous things. I do not know beneath which sky nor where you'll challenge fate; I only know that it will be high. I know the lives that *Mission Possible!* will touch for generations to come, and that you are great and each one of your people is great.

Wright

Well, those are great words to end on! We have come down to the bottom of our program; of course, Bonnie, I could talk to you all day, as I have done before.

We have been talking to Bonnie Libhart, former CEO of an international manufacturing corporation but now a unique professional speaker, trainer, and consultant, and she has written several books. And as we have found out, she is a very loving and intelligent person.

Bonnie, thank you so much for being on *Mission Possible!* today.

Libhart

Thank you for this opportunity, David.

About the Author

Dr. Bonnie Libhart's vision is to glorify God through the media. She is the host of a talk show called *Vision Plus*. Her message is distributed through TV, video, audio, the Internet, books, CDs, and DVDs. She also helps others write their memoirs. Dr. Libhart is the author of ten books, including her latest, *Spinning Silk*.

Dr. Bonnie Libhart
(877) 823-6886
www.DrBonnieLibhart.com

Chapter Five – Margie Wright

-

David Wright (D. Wright)

Today we are talking to Margie Wright, head coach of the Fresno State University softball program, a dynamic professional speaker and a published author who is nationally and internationally renowned. Ms. Wright is the NCAA's all-time winningest coach and led her team to a national title in 1998 while guiding the program to the NCAA Women's College World Series in ten of the last fifteen years. She has been featured in *USA Today*, showcased in *Sports Illustrated,* and featured in a book titled *Celebrating Women Coaches: A Biographical Dictionary.* Last fall she was inducted into the National Fastpitch Coaches Association's Hall of Fame. The previous fall she was inducted into the Illinois ASA Hall of Fame and the Fresno Athletic Hall of Fame. In addition, she was honored by the United States Olympic Committee as the 1998 USOC National Softball Coach of the Year.

Margie Wright, welcome to *Mission Possible!*

Margie Wright (M. Wright)

Thank you.

D. Wright

Ms. Wright, I had to reduce your introduction from eight pages, single-spaced, to a paragraph. Your achievements are "off the charts." What is the most personally satisfying accomplishment you have attained thus far in your life?

M. Wright

It's actually really difficult to pick one, but I've narrowed it down to three. One of them, for sure, is that in all the years I've been coaching, every young woman that has gone through my program for four years got a degree and is out in the world right now working as a professional and maybe even as a professional mom. They understood the concept of our philosophy, and they've all graduated. I think right along with that I'd have to include some winning accomplishments because that's what you do when you coach. Being part of winning the first gold medal for the United States in 1996 in the sport of softball was very important, and, of course, winning the National Championship in 1998 was extremely important, because we had finished second three times and third three times, so it was very gratifying to be able to win that.

D. Wright
Was that the first year that softball appeared in the Olympics?

M. Wright
Yes, in 1996.

D. Wright
And you coached the winning team?

M. Wright
I was an assistant coach, and the best part about it for me was I had five of my current and former players on the team, and it was in the United States. It was in Atlanta, and my family got to see it. Just the feeling you have when you are representing your country, in your own country where everyone is supportive of you and hoping you will win, is unbelievable. It was just an incredible experience.

D. Wright
Wow, I can imagine.
When you speak and train in the corporate world, do many of the methods and techniques you use as a coach apply to business people?

M. Wright
Yes, they really do, because I think coaching is somewhat of a business. You have someone in charge that is your leader, and if you're coaching a team sport, you have to work very hard to put a team together and to build people around a concept that will make your company or your team better. There are several qualities that you have to have as a manager. You have to be adaptable with all of your different employees; and when you have a team of fifteen to eighteen players, you certainly have to adapt to all of their different backgrounds. You have to be able to teach them to work together and to work with you as the person in charge, and it takes a lot of commitment.

It takes a lot of communication and a lot of self-discipline to be prepared every day that you go to work for the different crises that happen and the different attitudes that people can develop, depending on what's going on with them at home or within their relationships. You have to learn how to adapt to that in order to be able to make or to keep the business consistent and to keep your team players focused on the ultimate goal, which is to be the most successful company they can be.

D. Wright

You and I were talking last week, and I remember you telling me about all the accomplishments that have been made with the facilities in softball. You know, at most colleges, softball would be a very minor sport, wouldn't it?

M. Wright

Yes, that's true.

D. Wright

And didn't you say twenty-five hundred people attended your ballgames in a new stadium?

M. Wright

Yes, on an average when we play our rivalry teams, we've had as many as 6000, and our stadium holds close to 6000. We worked really hard to get this five-million-dollar stadium, and we were one of the first. A lot of schools have followed suit over the years, and it really has created a better environment for the female athletes to showcase their ability.

D. Wright

How does that affect your recruiting?

M. Wright

Well, it's kind of interesting. It affects it in a positive way, except young women don't care as much about facilities and fans when they go into college because there aren't any professional sports for them to look forward to. The most important things for them to look for in recruiting is the school and the academics and, of course, the softball program. The women who do get to play in our facility believe it's a dream come true for them, so in that way it does matter, but it doesn't matter quite as much as the academics and what the school has to offer.

D. Wright

Let me ask you about leadership. What do you think it takes to become an effective leader? In other words, are leaders born or developed?

M. Wright

I think it's a little bit of both. I feel that part of my leadership ability is something I was born with because of my parents, mostly because of what they had done and what they had been used to doing. Over the years I had to do something with those tools. I think some leaders may have the genes to be a leader, but a lot of people don't choose to go in that direction, so I'd have to say that the majority of leaders that I know are people that had to become developed leaders.

I think the number one quality that I recognize about people who are in leadership roles is their attitude. It is an extremely positive attitude. They never think that they can be beat. They never think that their company can't be the best that it can be. It's a different charisma that attracts quality people to them. I think that they have a lot of courage to step out to build a new business or build a team sometimes with less skilled people, yet they find a way to turn them into the best people they can be. They become very dependable people, and they have a clear understanding of the fact that if they're going to be a leader, they have to have a lot of integrity and they've got to be flexible. The fact that they have a positive attitude, a lot of self-respect, and have no problem respecting the people that work with them makes them great leaders.

D. Wright

Do you find a way to determine who your leaders are on your team there at your school?

M. Wright

The natural thing when you're dealing with people who compete is that leadership is going to come from your go-to person, the person that always comes through and has a natural, built-in sense of leadership. In past years I have had some players who were the go-to person, but they really didn't want anything to do with being the leader. I had to convince them that their leadership was not through what they had to say but more through being a role model and just doing the right things and letting other people catch on naturally. In competition, I think it's a little different from being in business, because they don't necessarily have to be the most outspoken—they just have to be the most focused, the people you go to when you need something to get done.

D. Wright

Many times in a company diverse cultures, different circumstances, and different belief systems make up the employee base. Still, companies have to work together to reach common goals. How do you go about teaching team building?

M. Wright

The first thing you do is recognize your leadership on your team. The teams that I've had in the past that haven't done very well have been the teams that had no one available to lead. Maybe they just don't want to do it, or they don't feel they have the qualities to show any kind of leadership. Sometimes what ends up happening at that point is the coach wants the team to do better than the team wants to do, and that doesn't work. Where I'm located, I have a tremendously diverse group of young women. We have a lot of people from wealthy backgrounds, yet the majority of our team is middle class. Because we are a part of the California State University system, our school is looked at as being "just a state school," and most times we get what I call "blue collar" kids. These young women have grown up with the concept of having to work hard for what they get.

I think if you're fortunate enough to have that kind of diversity, it's a little bit easier to train them to believe in something, to be great athletes. They already have in their minds what they want, what they want to do with it, and what they want to accomplish. That perseverance means they are not going to change their minds. I feel that I have been really lucky to be in the schools that I've been in, because it's been very easy to take each one of the players individually and express the team goals to them in a better way for them to understand. Ultimately, it's saying the same thing to fifteen different people; then it's a matter of getting the leadership on your team to follow you as the person in charge. It's a lot easier when you have more people going in the same direction as you. People who like to work hard understand getting on a leader's bandwagon.

D. Wright

I know. I get the pleasure of watching Pat Summit coach the University of Tennessee Lady Vols. Over at that big stadium we have some of the greatest ball teams come and play, coached by some fantastic women and men. In the women's coaching community, do you guys stick together? I mean, do you see each other often around the country?

M. Wright

Not really. I think we're all too busy to take the time, which is unfortunate. I don't really know that there is what I would call a "good old girls club," but, fortunately, I think women can be great advocates for each other. I think a lot of times, because of all the different responsibilities so many of the women coaches have, their time is really not their own, whereas many of the male coaches are married and have a support person at home, someone who helps them take care of the home and family. Female coaches, married or single, have that responsibility along with their coaching responsibility, so it's difficult to find adequate time to be able to share with other coaches.

D. Wright

That's a shame.

M. Wright

Yes, it really is.

D. Wright

Motivation seems to be a real problem in people today. Many business people complain about the inability to motivate their employees. Lack of enthusiasm seems to be rampant even among children and young people. What do you advise leaders to do to combat the lack of motivation?

M. Wright

I think there are a lot of different ways you can try to motivate, but they don't always work. You always have to be inventive and think of different things to try. One of the things I do first and foremost is ask my players to tell me what kinds of things motivate them, not just in softball but in life, in the classroom, and within their family. I ask them to tell me that, and even though they don't have an answer, they can give me a hint. Then I can design the motivation through different incentives to help fulfill what motivates them in their own minds. You can't sell somebody something they don't want to buy. It's impossible to do that. So in my motivation, the first thing I do is make them want to buy it. There are a lot of ways to do that, and every athlete that I've had is different. First, we try to take some of the pressure off of them individually and talk about the team motivation: How can they help the team be better? I have them help answer that question. Sometimes if they are just told what to do, that's not really any kind of motivation. That's just somebody fulfilling what somebody else wants them to do. I look at teaching them to motivate themselves more than telling them what to do. If they motivate themselves, they would automatically be motivating others within the team. You can't do that without self-respect, and you can't do that without recognizing the differences that everybody has within your team or within your business. Then you focus on the ones who are self-motivated and ask them, "Now this person is this way, so this isn't going to work. How can you help me motivate this person as your teammate?" You would be surprised how many positive answers you get and what they observe and recognize about each other. I think that instills personal motivation without even trying.

D. Wright
Were you raised in an environment conducive to personal growth and success awareness?

M. Wright
Absolutely. I couldn't have had a better opportunity to grow up. My family was, and still is, a phenomenal support system. My parents told me that I could do anything I wanted and that I had better believe it. From the day I was born, I felt like that was instilled in me. When I was ten, in my little town during the fifties and sixties, girls weren't really allowed to play sports. We had Little League teams, and all my friends that were boys wanted me to play on their Little League team because I was actually the best player. The father of one of my friends was the coach, so he let me play on the team and gave me a shirt. I was at the little village park getting ready to play in my first game, unaware that the Women's Club of our town was having a meeting across the street at the firehouse. Before the game even started, the Women's Club president came across the street and said, "You know what? We made a decision that girls can't play on the Little League teams." The Women's Club and the fire department all sponsored the Little League

programs, so it was their decision. I only lived a couple of blocks from the park, and I ran home crying the whole way. I'll bet I cried for three days. I couldn't get over the fact that they weren't going to let me play; that's all I wanted to do. My mom then told my dad that he needed to coach a girls team; he needed to start a girls team so I could play. So my older sisters and I played on a girls fast-pitch team that my dad coached. I did that for the first eight years of my softball life. Even though my dad worked two jobs, he found the time to be able to make sure that we got to compete. My mom would have done it except she had other kids and had to stay at home to take care of them. That right there told me that they were going to help me find a way to do whatever I wanted to do to pursue my dreams and to be able to grow as a young woman and use my talents.

D. Wright
Your dad sounds like quite a man.

M. Wright
Well, my dad and mom were both tremendous people. Just phenomenal people and very behind the scenes; nobody ever knew they were there. They never missed a game that I played in or many of the games that I coached in until my mom passed away. They would travel anywhere to support me. I kind of felt sorry for my siblings, because that took a lot of their time, but it was just something they were interested in. They knew that I had a special talent, and they just wanted to be a part of it. They are both very special people.

D. Wright
Do women have a greater struggle to achieve success than men in today's workplace? Or is the gender struggle simply different?

M. Wright
I definitely think women have a greater struggle, and the one area that I can relate to is athletics. I think women have so many other responsibilities. Young women who play sports are not going to sign a pro baseball, pro basketball, or pro football contract, so their schoolwork and their education is and has to be their number one priority. Not only do they have to excel on the field, they have to excel in the classroom. That takes a tremendous amount of time and focus. As a coach, I have to stay on it all the time to make sure my players are going to class and getting their assignments done, because they do

have to excel in both areas. I also think, based on our society, the media and everything else, a male athlete can get arrested and get thrown in jail and miss a few games, yet the fans can't wait for them to get back on the court or on the field so they can support them no matter what. A woman athlete would never be able to do that and would never be taken in with open arms. So I think society makes it more difficult as well. Usually, if you're a female who's successful in athletics, people look at you a little bit differently because they don't like to be challenged by successful women.

For so many years in our society, sports have revolved around men and male athletes. Women face more difficult challenges. When they become more successful than the male coaches, it is tough. When you're successful, you feel like you can demand better facilities and demand a better salary. But when you make those demands, you get looked upon as being just a demanding female. Also, a man can get fired from one job and get paid more money to go to another job and be taken in without any problems. Not a woman. There's no question that it's more of a struggle on the job as well as dealing with all the other responsibilities that many women coaches have at home.

D. Wright
Coach Wright, with our *Mission Possible!* talk show and book, we are trying to encourage people in our audience to be better, live better and be more fulfilled by listening to the examples of our guests. Is there anything or anybody in your life that has made a difference for you and helped you to be a better person?

M. Wright
I'd have to say there were four people. Both of my parents, without a doubt, as I said before. They gave me the drive to go after anything I wanted in life. I will always be grateful to them. But I had a college basketball coach and also a summer softball coach who really made a difference in my life. My summer softball coach, who volunteered her time, was a very quiet woman who believed more in me than I believed in myself. That is something that I had to learn from her. She would not let me doubt myself. When you compete and fail, it is easy to question your ability, your drive, and everything else. She never let me do that for the ten years that I played under her, and I will always be grateful for that.

The fourth person was my college basketball coach, who was also my softball coach for a couple of years when I first got to college. I went to college primarily to play sports, because there weren't any high school sports for girls. The only way I could play basketball competitively was to go to college to play. I got to be a starter as a freshman, but I was used to playing on the playground against all of my guy friends. A lot goes on at the playground; you have to kill or be killed when you're out there with a bunch of guys, so I developed a little bit of a temper and a very feisty attitude on the court. I remember the first game that I showed my temper, the coach pulled me out of the game and sat me down beside her and told me if I ever acted like that again, I'd never play another game. That woke me up quickly. Then later on, when we were at the College World Series and she was my softball coach, we were getting ready to play the championship game, and I remember her asking me a difficult question. She said, "Now listen, the only way we're going to beat them is if you as the pitcher can change your speeds around—you know, have four or five different speeds." I looked at her and said, "I've never done that before." And she said, "Yes, but you could do it, couldn't you?" And I said, "Yes, ma'am, I can do it." I went out into the outfield, and the catcher and I practiced for twenty minutes. We went into the game and it worked! It was definitely something that worked because she made me believe I could do it. She was my coach and I respected her, so I was going to find a way to overachieve and do that for her and our team.

I really have a great deal of admiration for those four people, because I think that's why I am where I am today.

D. Wright

When you consider the choices you've made down through the years, has faith played an important role in your life?

M. Wright

Oh, most definitely. I don't think I could be where I am without having, first of all, a very strong belief in God and just a very strong belief in people and in myself. I think that what faith has allowed me to do is to know there is always a solution and an answer. Because I believe that, whatever I decide I want my team to be able to do, I'm able to walk the walk and be consistent with that because of that very strong belief in everything about my life. When you have faith in yourself, it's easy to portray that to other people, especially young people who at times have a very difficult time believing in anything.

D. Wright

People are fascinated with these new TV shows about being a survivor. What has been the greatest comeback from adversity in your career or in your life?

M. Wright

I would have to say a couple of things. One was the year that my mother passed away. We were at the end of our season when she died on April 30, a week before our regionals. That was a real struggle. I missed ten games because I was 2100 miles away and had to fly back and forth during the season. That year we weren't ranked very high, but we made it to the College World Series and finished second, one game away from winning the whole thing. It was very difficult to come back and coach my team to that success. I will always be affected by that. My dad has been ill this spring, and it's been a difficult time just wanting to be at home yet having the responsibility of my team and his wanting me to be with my team. I think those are very difficult times, when the people that mean the most to you are struggling or when it's a life-or-death situation; that's very difficult to come back from.

A struggle I went through professionally was when our school was investigated. The Office of Civil Rights came to Fresno State and investigated us to find out if we were in compliance with treating male and female athletes the same. When they came here, they found that we were out of compliance in eleven of the thirteen areas, and in a community like this, where athletics is the number one form of entertainment, there are going to be people taking sides. The newspaper and Fresno State male coaches and administration publicly painted a picture that women didn't deserve to be equal. Since I was the most successful women's coach on campus and had been here the longest, I became the target for everybody who was against Title IX. They had to build a softball stadium, even though we had to go raise money to pay the loan back and the community really was not supportive of us. There was a radio talk show host that hated Title IX, and he did a two-hour talk show bashing me and bashing Title IX. The university would not step in, so I eventually had to file a lawsuit. It lasted over a two-year time period and got to the point where I couldn't even afford my lawyer fees. I even had to start putting my house up for sale because I couldn't pay for everything. I believed strongly that the women should be treated fairly, and I believed strongly that the radio host had no right to paint that picture of me. In fact, the lawsuit was settled out of court, which basically was a huge victory for me and all women. It was a moral victory, and it definitely sent the message to the community that it was the right thing to do, to help the women be equal to the men without cutting the men's sports financially.

Then that following year, we won the national championship. At that time, everybody in that community loved us! But it was a very difficult time. I was offered a lot of different jobs at very good schools, and I probably should have taken them, but in my mind I wasn't going to let them drive me out of a program that I had built. If I was going to change jobs, it was going to be on my terms and not on the terms of a bunch of spoiled male coaches and people in the community that just couldn't stand the fact that the women were equal to the men and deserved to be treated equally.

Those were two things that I survived that I didn't think I ever would.

D. Wright

If you could have a platform and tell our audience something you feel would help or encourage them, what would you say?

M. Wright

I would tell them, first and foremost, that life is short, and they need to get everything that they can out of their talents, out of their abilities, and out of the person that they are. They should love themselves and take care of themselves first, because if they do that, it's much easier to lead other people. I would tell them to always try to find the good in everybody and everything, even though in life there are some negatives. They need to find a way to turn negatives into positives and recognize that within our short lives there's always a way to win. It doesn't mean winning by score. It means that there's always a way to become the best person we can be; and if we just take advantage of that, in this very difficult world that we live in, it's easy to go in the right direction. So if I had anything to say, it would be to go for being the best you can be and never let anything stand in the way.

D. Wright

Well, this has been a fast thirty minutes. I really appreciate your talking to me. I know it's early out there on what we call the Left Coast.

We have been talking to Margie Wright, head coach of the Fresno State University softball program. She's also a dynamic professional speaker and published author, who is nationally and internationally renowned.

Ms. Wright, thank you so much for being a guest on *Mission Possible!* today.

M. Wright
Thank you.

About the Author

Head coach Margie Wright is the NCAA's all-time winningest coach in Division I softball and is in her 18th season at the helm of the Fresno State softball program. Wright became the first Division I softball coach to record 1000 Division I victories last year. The 1998 NCAA National Coach of the Year boasts a 24-year career record of 1051-363-3 (.743). Wright has recorded thirteen 50-win campaigns and has averaged 52 wins

Margie Wright
c/o Fresno State Softball
631 Houston Avenue
Clovis, CA 93611
Office: (559) 278-4453
Secretary: (559) 278-6833

Chapter Six – Tim Sanders

-

David Wright (Wright)

Today we are talking to Tim Sanders, Yahoo!'s chief solutions officer. He is a seasoned sales professional charged with delivering next-generation marketing programs to world class brands. Tim joined Yahoo! as part of the acquisition of Broadcast.com in 1999. Tim's dynamic presentation skills have made him a highly respected speaker at executive level conferences and graduate schools. He is the author of *Love Is the Killer App,* published by Random House. His best-selling book has been endorsed by Stephen Covey, Tom Peters, Seth Godin, Phil McGraw, and Faith Popcorn.

Tim Sanders, welcome to *Mission Possible!*

Tim Sanders (Sanders)

Well, thank you.

Wright

I've read your book, and in it you write about your client, Victoria's Secret. You stated that you committed yourself to an unholy alliance with America Online and Microsoft. Tell us about this kind of sharing.

Sanders

Just for our listeners, let me give a little background. There was the 1999 Victoria's Secret Fashion Show webcast—you know, the one that brought the Internet to its knees. We're talking now about the second one, in 2000, that was supposed to work—and it did work, as a matter of fact. In that situation, I had a lot of compassion for my client, Victoria's Secret. I really wanted this to work; but to make it happen, I was going to have to open up the network and cooperate with people that we formerly competed with, or still compete with. This happens all the time in good business. I'm sure the Olympics is the biggest compromise in the world between networks and between cable and broadcast, to make it all work for everybody's interests. This is the same thing; I had to involve and coordinate with America Online and Microsoft for MSN so that the second event would be successful. There is tremendous risk in doing that; I could have lost the business.

Wright

The first webcast I remember; of course, I think we all remember more about the first one than we do the second one. Was the problem just too many calls?

Sanders

Yes. I mean, too many people wanted it, and it stressed too many Internet service providers who themselves were new to the game—you know, the local ISPs. The system wasn't quite big enough to broadcast an event with that much viewership. The second time it happened, a couple of things had occurred for us. I won't get technical, but we were able to multicast and dramatically increase the capacity, so the second one worked wonderfully. It worked wonderfully for America Online users as well as users of the Microsoft network, because everybody cooperated. And again, that was a situation of my looking at the business relationship, thinking I would rather have the client successful than have the client.

Wright

That's right; I read that in your book. I also read that everyone looked at the first project as a negative, but the client, Victoria's Secret, looked at it as a real positive.

Sanders

Sure. They gathered well into a half-million e-mail addresses with permission to send the catalog digitally, and that became a huge database of people who wanted to receive the catalog and then bought against that e-mail. They make a lot of money on that now. But whether or not people could get online is what you heard about. I would estimate that somewhere north of five hundred million people globally heard about that between the good news and the bad news. You know how publicity is; it's all good. It didn't fail because they did anything wrong. But with all that being said, when I looked at that situation, I felt like, "Whew, we got out by the skin of our teeth. It's a good thing we collected a lot of data." The commitment was, the second time we do this we've got to do better—"we" meaning Broadcast.com and Yahoo! As a supplier to a client, we have to do better, because if you heard about it twice, you only heard it once right. If you heard about it twice, my belief was that it would begin to hurt them.

Wright

You also stated in your book that the most important facet of building a brand is to differentiate your person, product, or service. Tell us what you mean by that.

Sanders

As Jack Welch would say, "You've got to jump out of the pile." Whether you're talking about a person inside a huge company with a lot of other people, or whether you're talking about a detergent lined up on a grocery shelf with hundreds of other detergents, it's all about a pile. Everybody's world is cluttered. People who get ahead in their careers jump out of the pile; they're different. Same thing for brands like Starbucks. They just jumped out of the pile, and people prefer it now. You've got to differentiate yourself with something. You want it to be good, right? You don't want to differentiate yourself like our friend Kenneth Lay has differentiated himself. You want to differentiate yourself for being a nice, smart person; and if you do that, you became very unique, very rare, very cherished, and better things happen.

Wright

I had a negative attitude toward Starbucks when I first saw their prices, but then, the coffee was great! So now the prices make absolutely no difference to me.

Sanders

That's right. If you're different, people will pay whatever it costs. I've also noticed that it works the same way with people. If people prefer you, they don't care. There's a story I always think about—it's not in the book, but it's a story about a guy named Elmer Letterman. Have you ever heard about him?

Wright

No.

Sanders

He's no relationship to David Letterman. He was an insurance salesperson in the twenties, right before the Great Depression. He was a crazy guy, but what he would do is book a table for four every Friday at the Manhattan Four Seasons. He would prospect all week, and on

Friday he'd put together three other business people that should meet. He did tremendous introductions for business opportunities every Friday at lunch. He'd pay the bill, and he never sold insurance. If you asked him at the table about insurance, he would say, "You'll have to call my partner next week; that's not why we're here. We're here because you should meet." Just imagine; this guy does this a solid fifty weeks out of the year for a solid ten years. He's running the place in New York by the thirties. He's a multimillionaire. You know why? Because who else are these people going to do business with at any price? Elmer made them successful. He never tried to collect on the debt. People overpay that type of karma. Elmer learned the Dale Carnegie thing. Dale Carnegie looked at the situation and in 1935 released the book *How to Win Friends and Influence People,* and he said to Elmer's nod, "You will get more done in two months developing a sincere interest in two people than you will ever accomplish in two years trying to get two people interested in you." And that's what that's about.

Wright
That's brilliant.

Sanders
And Elmer gets paid retail or better, because he adds value, which is the key.

Wright
Right.

Sanders
And differentiating is adding value.

Wright
Tim, as I read your book, you seemed to take customer satisfaction to a new level. You talked about the cost of attracting a new customer being five times the cost of keeping a current customer happy. You also talked about customer tenure. Could you explain how all this works?

Sanders
If you lose customers, you spend an incredible amount of money to get new customers or, God forbid, bring back these original

customers. If you focus on servicing the existing customers, you always have lower costs, higher profit, and more velocity in your business, meaning you turn over your business much faster because they are just replenishing.

The interesting thing about keeping customers is that they're the best receivers for your advertising. I want you to think about this: Let's say that you are a huge Nike fan and you buy Nike shoes. Every time you see a Nike television commercial, you are thirteen times more likely to notice and pay three seconds of attention to it than if you were not a Nike customer, because if you are not buying that brand, you've learned how to filter out the messaging of buying— although sometimes it pops through. If you don't buy a particular brand, the advertising just bounces off of you; but if you buy that brand, you pay attention to the advertising, and guess what you do? You go out and buy another pair of Nike shoes. Nike is very powerful because they can do that.

Now, customer tenure just means that the longer I'm a customer with you, the more likely I am to be a profitable customer. If I buy something from you at Nordstrom's, which is a great customer service company, and I return the first two items because I know that you will take anything back, then you will lose money on me as a customer until I have a tenure of about a year and fifteen transactions. But then you will start to make money. Grocery stores live on this. You can spend a hundred bucks and they'll make a buck fifty on you. Seriously. But over the course of time, if you join their frequency program and buy high-margin items that they discount, they will make three dollars every time they see you, five dollars every time they see you, and then you will be worth a thousand bucks a year to them over the course of time. That's how they grow it. But if you jump around from company to company where you buy, or if you jump around from company to company where you work, you don't have much value.

Wright

You know, it always makes me feel good when I see a brand that I buy advertising on television. It reminds me one more time of how brilliant I am.

Sanders

It does. And you know another thing they do? They suddenly educate you on how to get the benefits out of the product you're holding in your hand. Let me give you an example: "Coke . . . it's refreshing." You know, that's the last thing you think before you take a sip of it. You're sitting there with a Coke in your hand and a TV commercial runs and a smile comes across your face. It's been seen in focus groups; you take a sip of it because you've just been educated one more time: It's refreshing. That's advertising that adds value. If you advertise benefits and help the consumer enjoy what they've already bought, that's tremendous. Think about AOL. AOL educates and they've used their own network to market this. They educate you on all the things they have: "It's so easy to use, no wonder it's number one." That's for the existing customer. It's continuing to remind you, "Hey, did you know you have this, you have chat, you can do instant messaging, you can do photos?" That's interesting to me.

Wright

A couple of decades ago, I began reading a lot of business self-help books. I never heard so many buzzwords in my life, but you write about some things that really are, if not unique, at least thought provoking. You write about "bislove" as being the act of intimacy. You also talk about being a "lovecat," which I found very interesting. Could you define *bislove* and *lovecat*?

Sanders

The reason I use phrases like that is to provoke you. Sometimes buzzwords are used because people are trying to take concepts that are common, unique, everyday things that everybody already knows, and they're going to put some buzzwords around them, and they're going to own a new idea. I gave up on new ideas a long time ago. I figured I wasn't going to have a new idea with the book, but I was hoping that I would be a voice for other people who would read the book and say, "Wow, this is how I live."

So with that being said, here are the two definitions: *Bislove* is short for business love. (I was just thinking how Sammy Davis Jr. would say it: "Bislove, baby.") Business love is very unique because, remember, you have a social contract to add value at your company. So whatever you do to love other people as a business person had better be good for the company you work for, or it's not very loving to the company. It's a required balance. So *business love* is defined as the intelligent sharing of your intangibles—your knowledge, your network, your compassion—to promote growth and success in other people, whether it's your customer or your colleagues or your supplier. So when you share your knowledge and your network and your compassion with somebody to help make them successful and to grow them, that's business love.

Now *lovecat*—I love the term because it provokes people, it freaks people out when I call them lovecat. Mostly men will say, "Oh, my God, what are you saying, boy?" But it's from a Cure song in the '80s. Robert Smith was the lead singer of The Cure, and he wrote the lyrics that open the song: "We move like cagey tigers, we couldn't get closer than this." I thought about that while I was trying to find a word for nice, smart business people, and I love the word *lovecat*.

When I say lovecat, I mean that this person is the most generous person with knowledge you have ever met. You think they're reading in their spare time for your benefit, they're that on-point. They always have a Rolodex handy to put you in touch with the exact person you need to meet, and they disappear when they put you together. You scratch your head wondering how they're going to let you take advantage of them. And they differentiate, because they are incredibly personable. They're shrewd. Lovecats are incredibly shrewd. They're pay-me-retail, make-a-profit business people, but they will walk up to you, put their arm around you, and say, "You know what? I really appreciate you. I love you." And you scratch your head, like people did with Herb Kelleher at Southwest Airlines: "How can you pay that way?" The answer is because you built your foundation on knowledge, you accented it with network, and you put an exclamation point with your compassion. The lovecat thing for me is that in a dog-eat-dog world, I choose to be a cat. I love cats, you know?

Wright
Right.

Sanders
I used to think about this when I was growing up: There was this big huge German shepherd, a big, big, big, bad dog, and this little, itty-bitty Siamese cat. I'll never forget watching that big dog chase that little cat across the backyard until that chain would go taut and that dog's neck would jerk back and the cat would laugh. I would think, If that dog ever gets hold of that cat, it's over. He never did, though. In business, it's the same concept. You can be a mad dog, just like the German shepherd. You don't have to be all that intelligent; you just have to be protective and, most importantly, distrust people. You will still get fed at the end of the day, and it may look to the outside world like you're incredibly happy. But for me, I take the harder, more

uncertain, freer road of being the cat. Cats have value because they're intelligent and agile. If they were stupid and slow, they'd be dog food, right? Business life is about a choice that you make and about the type of person that you are. You believe either in scarcity or abundance. You believe either there's not enough or there's enough to go around. We can't plod along in life saying, I'm neither fish nor fowl; work isn't personal. That's a cop-out, I say, and you will be incredibly unhappy when you retire if you live like that.

Wright

Very interesting. It seems to me that you write about the importance of knowledge more than any other subjects. You say that people should accumulate enough knowledge that they can share it with others. What happened to corporate secrecy?

Sanders

Remember, I always think of intangibles being intelligently shared; so when I talk about knowledge, I'm saying it is the foundation to my business house. Think about it as a pyramid, and think of the bottom half of the pyramid, the foundation, as knowledge. In other words, the first impression people are going to have about me is that I'm incredibly knowledgeable in things they're interested in, and I'm generous with that knowledge. It's not required that I share corporate secrets to add value and knowledge. Let's say emotional intelligence is interesting to you as a professional marketer, and I've read three books on the issue and studied it carefully over a few weeks. When I talk to you about that, I'm going to educate you and make you more successful. That's powerful stuff. I don't have to tell you company secrets to make that type of impression on you. Remember "nice plus smart." Nice plus smart people succeed. It's just profoundly different—that's the answer. Go spend your spare time stockpiling public domain knowledge, stuff that is in bookstores, in libraries or on-line, for the benefit of other people, and give it to them, because your company doesn't own that. This is what you own outright, your own personal intangibles.

Wright

Before, you were telling us about the man who reserved the four seats at the Four Seasons. I guess that was networking before we really called it networking.

Sanders
Right.

Wright
Could you tell us the difference between networking and business matchmaking?

Sanders
Sure. Well, actually the distinction I like to make is the difference between networking and brokering. To me, business matchmaking and networking is the idea that I put two people together that should meet, and I have no expectation for myself personally. I mean, I do it because they should meet and I know it's going to add value, and that's what business matchmaking is. You're like a little corporate Yenta—you like putting people together because you think it makes sense. You've got an incredibly good taste and hunch about this, and it always seems to work. That's just talent. Now brokering is different. Brokering is when somebody says, "I can get you a job somewhere." And so they get you a job and they hassle you for two years to do something nice for them because they got you the damn job. That's brokering, because there's a price to pay. Or somebody says, "I want you, the restaurant entrepreneur, to meet my friend, the venture capitalist; when you two do a deal and drop paperwork, you give me ten thousand shares." That is not networking; that is brokering.

Wright
Right.

Sanders
And when you put a price on your love like that, then people see you coming later. They know there's a cost to you. Sometimes it's an unwritten cost. That's the scariest one, right? It's priceless how much it costs to work with you, so God forbid they shrug away from your recommendations over time and they never introduce people to you. God forbid you work with them like that.

What I've learned is that our personal networking works just like the Internet. Think about when the Internet first came out. What was everyone so excited about (and it's still true to this day)? It is the idea that the Internet takes some friction out of getting things from manufacturers, right? They put the manufacturers directly in contact with the customer and took friction out of the system. It reduced costs. It eliminated the middle person.

I think the same thing happens in the real life. When you share your network with no expectations, people are just surprised and delighted. It's like a branding event. They always listen to your recommendations because there is no cost to listening to you; and the fact that you are so generous with your network makes them want to introduce you to their network and you begin to grow exponentially just like the Internet did because there is no friction.

So I think the Internet really is a metaphor of how we are in business. I think the Internet is just the result of society; it's not something that drives society. It's a symptom, not a cure. We are the ones that have the power. Networking is true, and the Internet was based on the human experience.

Wright

I was really surprised at my own behavior. I swore I would never buy anything off the Internet simply because I wouldn't know the people, but I bought a computer. It arrived and didn't work, so I was happy that they had messed up. I thought, Now they're going to hassle me. I called, and they said that something must have happened in shipping, and the next day I got another computer. I thought to myself, How did they do that? If I'd gone down to a computer store, I could have gotten that kind of service. So it's really great buying on-line, and you're right—it does reduce the middle person, the friction, and, in my case, it lowered the cost.

Sanders

Well, let's point something out too. Did they surprise and delight you that it showed up the next day?

Wright

Absolutely!

Sanders

If you had to look at it in the dollars-and-cents value to you, in terms of doing business with them over time, it's priceless. There's a great story of a lady in her eighties who went to Nordstrom's one day and asked to get her money back on her tires because she felt like they sold her the wrong type of tires. One of the Nordstrom brothers immediately looked at the situation, wrote her a check for the difference, and then found somebody locally who actually sold tires (because they didn't). But because the lady was a long-time customer, they had compassion on her; she was just confused. You do those types of things to create surprise and delight, just like you network people like Elmer Letterman did, with no expectations, in order to create that same "Aha, what a great company! What a great person!"

Wright

Tim, with our *Mission Possible!* talk show and book, we are trying to encourage people in our audience to be better, live better, and be more fulfilled by listening to the examples of our guests. Is there anyone or anything in your life that has made a difference for you and helped you to be a better person?

Sanders

I've surely had a lot over the course of my life, but given the nature of our particular talk, I'll chose one. His name is Mark Cuban. Many of you might know him as the founder of Broadcast.com and currently the owner of the Dallas Mavericks—a very boisterous young man and a fabulously successful businessperson. When I went to work for him, I learned something new about customer service. Mark was a fanatic about customers being happy with service. He was known to answer any e-mail that went to any problem, suggestion, or support e-mail box at Broadcast.com. The corporate motto for service was "Make love, not war." He would just go bonkers if anybody had a bad experience. He always said that the best way to predict future earnings is to ask the customers how happy they are with the service. That's profound. I had been in many businesses (I don't care what they said on their little PowerPoint presentations) that basically said the customers were liars and the employees were worse. Mark was quite the opposite. That was really interesting to me, to really feel that way about customers, and, of course, that's what led to the style of business that people saw in the Victoria's Secret Fashion Show. It brings us full circle. I was under Mark's tutorage at that time and I acted like it: Make love, not war.

Wright

What do you think makes up a great mentor? In other words, are there characteristics that mentors seem to have in common?

Sanders

I think there are, but, fundamentally, a great mentor takes great satisfaction in the progress of other people. They directly enjoy and feed on other people's success. If you can't do that, you're not going to be a good mentor. If you are, instead, vicarious and have to own a piece of it for yourself, or if you're calculating so that it's all about a business, about making more money at the end of the day, then you're going to have a very inconsistent experience, because mentoring doesn't always work out to be profitable, and it doesn't always have to be about you. So the vicarious and the insincere people will have a bad experience, but the people who are sincere and take incredible delight in other people's progress are the ones who are going to be the best mentors.

Wright

That would fit perfectly into your "no expectations" theory.

Sanders

Right. People ask me what I get out of doing a book. I get great conversations like you and I are having today. I get dozens of e-mails every day at tim@timsanders.com, and I take great delight in those. I don't say, "Oh, did you buy the book?" It doesn't matter. We're having an incredibly cool conversation, and I take delight out of it, especially if it's benefiting you.

Wright

Most people are fascinated with the new TV shows about being a survivor. What has been the greatest comeback you have made from adversity in your career or life?

Sanders

My best comeback was when I re-entered the business world in 1990 after being on the road five years as a reggae musician. After graduate school, I fell off the edge of the earth and did a walkabout, as they call it in Australia, for a few years as a musician. The bus broke down in Dallas, Texas, and I was given a really interesting job assignment (actually, this was 1986) with Southwestern Bell Mobile Systems, when cellular phones were first rolled out to the public, before they were even called wireless phones. That was literally my first comeback, if you will. Life is a series of comebacks. I've had more since then, but that one was profound for me, because I had been raised through high school and college to have such great potential. I'm sure I disappointed my mama, but I came back, and I came back by getting involved in a brand-new business that required customer service.

Wright

When you consider the choices you have made down through the years, has faith played an important role in your life?

Sanders

I think so; I hope so. I try to evoke every single day. I've had to have a lot of faith, because I practice the invisible, meaning that now I give away and value myself based on things that I can't add up, like how much knowledge I have. How do I put a number on that? Yes, my whole life is based on faith. You could just imagine a guy like me writing a book that says, "Hey, nice, smart people succeed." I had to have a lot of faith that there are other people out there that I'm talking to that make a resumé with this.

Wright

Yes, I think this book is going to be a great seller. I also like Brian Tracy's book *Get Paid More and Promoted Faster.* He basically agrees with you. He says, "Work hard and be nice." It's kind of simple when you get right down to it.

Sanders

It's kind of interesting, don't you think? One of the things that I learned about being a writer is that you don't write to make up great ideas, necessarily. Kurt Vonnegut said that in a world with hundred-million-dollar movies and billion-dollar theme parks, you can't help but wonder why people even read at all, and why we write. But he said the reason that we write is because we want to let the reader know that there is somebody else out there that's thinking the same thoughts.

Wright
Right.

Sanders

And that they're not alone. I think that's why we write. I think that when a writer writes, thinking they're going to change the world, it's not a very good book.

Wright

That's right. I noticed that some of the words you are using, you give other people credit for in your book.

Sanders

Oh, absolutely. You've got to give credit where credit is due.

Wright

If you could have a platform and tell our audience something you feel would help or encourage them, what would you say?

Sanders

I would say, Stop hurting people; just stop hurting. As I've toured the country, I have found that for some folks, with their time constraints, it's very difficult to figure out how to read a book a week. And even if they read that much, who do they talk to on a regular basis? The same goes for the network: Who do they know? How are they going to make a difference? Sometimes people say, "I'm not a touchy-feely person. I'm a distrusting person; I've been hurt." But I look at all those things and say that you don't have to be a god; just stop hurting people. We don't need to be so hateful. We can't act pious and say we don't do that; yes, we do. The average person says the word *hate* when referring to another person over four dozen times a month, and they say *love* when referring to another person less than a dozen times a month. This is on average, of course, so it may vary. Maybe it's all about what Leo Buscaglia said when he wrote the book *Love*. (What a fabulous guy, right?) He said that words are like reality, and that the way to change your life is to choose a day, such as next Monday, and every time you're about to say the word *hate*, rephrase it—use the word *love* instead and your life will change.

Wright

We have come to the end of a half hour. Can you believe that?

Sanders

Hey, hey, hey!

Wright

Today we've been talking to Tim Sanders, Yahoo!'s chief solutions officer. He is the author of a new book entitled *Love Is the*

Killer App, and I would think that you would do well to go out and get a copy, whether you're in business or not. This is one great book and a great guy.

Tim, I appreciate your being on our program this morning.

Sanders
Well, I had a great time with you, and I hope you have a swank day and go do something nice for somebody; and when they say, "What's gotten into you?" you can say, "This love thing is getting to me."

Wright
I'll say, "I've talked to Tim Sanders this morning."

Sanders
That's great!

Wright
Tim, thank you so much.

Sanders
Thank you.

About the Author

Prior to leading the solutions team, Tim Sanders created and led the Yahoo! ValueLab, an in-house "think tank" that delivers value-added propositions to prospective and current Yahoo! clients.

The team which Sanders built continues to serve as a consultation practice for clients, by coordinating and leveraging Yahoo!'s resources to find, connect with and add value to clients' growth strategies.

Tim Sanders
(408) 910-7857
tsanders@yahoo-inc.com

Chapter Seven – Dr. Joanne Sujansky

David E. Wright (Wright)

Today we're talking to Dr. Joanne Sujansky, Certified Speaking Professional. She is a business owner and international professional speaker, author, and consultant. Focus, intense passion, and effort have earned her a doctorate degree. Joanne earned the distinction of becoming the youngest National President ever in the history of the American Society for Training and Development (ASTD), a seventy thousand member professional organization. Also, because of her outstanding performance in and contribution to the training and development field, ASTD awarded Joanne their highest honor, the Gordon M. Bliss Award. Having delivered services throughout the United States and across the globe, Joanne has built her training, consulting, and assessment company, KEYGroup®, to a prominent position in the training field. Because of her incredible professional platform skills, she has spoken in thirty countries and has earned the distinction of Certified Speaking Professional (CSP). This prestigious title has only been given to less than eight percent of the National Speakers Association's (NSA) four thousand members.

Joanne Sujansky, welcome to *Mission Possible!*

Joanne Sujansky (Sujansky)

Thank you very much, David.

Wright

Joanne, tell our listeners and readers a little about your newest book, *The Keys to Conquering Change: 100 Tales of Success.* I understand that this book contains one hundred stories of people who have changed their lives for the better. What insights did you gain from interviewing these people?

Sujansky

David, it was really quite a lot of fun to interview so many people with very diverse life changes. People ranging in age from fourteen to eighty told these stories. It was so interesting to talk to people from all walks of life, from six or seven different countries. We asked these individuals to reflect on major changes in their lives, how they coped with them, and what they learned. Sometimes we knew ahead of time about major changes some of these people had been through, and we expected them to talk about those specific changes. But they often surprised us and talked about different ones. They were really open and looking forward to talking to us. We changed the individuals' names for the book because we were worried about identifying them since many mentioned bosses, family members, and so on.

We heard later that people were disappointed because they wanted to read their names and be recognized for what they accomplished. Through their stories, we confirmed that, of course, imposed and unexpected change is the hardest kind, and that people really surprised themselves with what they were able to get through. When they heard about the imposed change, or when they knew what they were soon going to face, they were shocked, frightened, even concerned about their ability to deal with it. However, most managed to overcome the odds even when they weren't sure, initially, that they could.

Wright
Are you talking about circumstantial change?

Sujansky
I'm talking about all kinds of change. We talked to people whose organizations had been downsized. We talked to people who had been through anything from a divorce, a new relationship, or the birth of a child with special challenges. One story was about a woman who sat down to dinner with her five children and her 38-year-old husband only to have her husband die right at the table. The types of changes and situations were varied. After going through these changes, people felt that they wouldn't sweat the small stuff in the future and that the skills they learned would help them through more of life's changes in the future. Most people said they were initially paralyzed by the change, but usually they rallied, found the supports that they needed, and got it together. Then they were awfully proud of themselves that they had made it through the change.

Wright
Did writing the book start out as a business venture and end up being more personal for you?

Sujansky

For many years I have worked in the areas of leadership and change and have taught the theories that I learned in my graduate program, as well as some things that I learned in life. I had talked to people in the corporate environment but had never pulled people away from the business world and asked them about both their business and personal changes. I never before had the opportunity to give people a chance to talk so much about what they did and what they learned or what skills they developed through the process. For instance, many people talked about not knowing how much they *did* need help. Reaching out to a special friend, to someone with different skills, or to a professional person was really empowering for them and helped them through the change process.

We've always talked about the fact that partnering through change makes it easier and more successful. That was one of the things that some people discovered. Others discovered that they really had to stay focused, since there were a lot of distractions and a lot of things that gave them problems through the change process. They had to stay focused on where they were going and see the picture in their minds of what it could be. Some people experienced such tragic losses that they had no mental picture of life without that person. They really had to recreate and reinvent their futures. As they learned to do that and successfully accomplished it, they were really proud of themselves and proud to tell their stories.

Wright

I remember talking to you two or three months ago. You stated then that your book might serve as a guide for managers and employees who are recovering from 9/11 and its effects on the workplace. Tell me a little more about what you meant.

Sujansky

It was very interesting. The book came out, and a local paper writing about the events of that week called me and interviewed me about the book and its relevance to people going through this horrific change. As I said, David, I really hadn't planned to write the book with that in mind, but we saw the workforce full of a lot of feelings of loss and fear. Throughout the world people had feelings of loss and fear. Downsizing was already happening, and then it happened more. The economy was tough and getting tougher. One of the things that really seemed to help managers was understanding the need to help people stay focused. For some, it was the need to get refocused, and managers had the responsibility to help people do just that. Managers needed to acknowledge that times were tough and that people would not get over it quickly. They needed to acknowledge out loud that they understood it was a painful and confusing time. We thought that the managers who did that were more real and more believable. They served as really strong leaders through the tough times. The business needed to be made clearer to people; they needed to see a future in the business—where it was going, what it would be. They also needed to let people know that there was hope for the future, when possible.

Managers needed to help employees build alliances, both inside their workplaces and outside. Alliances or support systems were needed to help them do their jobs better, but also they were necessary to help them through life.

Daily priorities needed to be clearer. I notice, as a person who works with corporate leaders over long periods of time, that changes happen often, with priorities shifting often. Sometimes the leaders in the organization are aware of these changing priorities, but it's questionable whether or not the employees understand it. When we're in a state of flux, it is important to be dynamic and able to handle that change, but sometimes managers are not clear about priorities. There needs to be more of that. I think certainly we see a greater demand for a work/life balance. Perhaps this need is greater now because people are saying, "Hey, life really is too short." We're coaching managers and leaders to understand that work is a part of life.

Wright

When you address people that we would call leaders, you have said many times they don't really prepare for change; therefore, their employees don't cope well. How do you suggest that leaders better prepare for change?

Sujansky

I think that, for the most part, in corporations that are strong and dynamic, people are clear about where the company is going. They see the vision and they have a good idea of what it is, but in a lot of places that's not true. I tell leaders that they need to shape and share the corporate vision so that it's real to people. Be visible and approachable to the people that work inside your company. I think some of the strongest leaders are people who are around once in a while and people know they can approach them. I think that there's not enough soliciting of input from people who have real talent and real ideas about what could help the company and what could make it stronger. I think that as leaders prepare for change, which is constant, they need to solicit input and really hear what people are saying.

When a big change is coming, people want to know what will stay the same. It's really interesting—sometimes when I say that in a keynote speech, I see some very key people in the room writing that down. It is helpful to know what *won't* change, not only what's going to change. We feel some security when we know some things will be the same.

I think leaders make the mistake of thinking that people will react the same way to change as they do. That seems kind of silly, when you think about it, because we're all so different. I react to change based on my experiences in life and based on my resources right now. How I feel today will determine how I react to change today. I think one of the things we need to know as leaders is that everyone around us has a very personalized, very individual reaction to the change process, and we need to respect that. People need a lot of information throughout the change process, but sometimes the opposite happens. Leaders are busy, leaders are in meetings, leaders are shaping and making the change, and so they're not communicating as much as they need to. Then the grapevine fills in the blanks.

Wright

So if I intend to be a great leader of my company, I would do well to remind my employees of the things that won't change in our organization—things like integrity, moral standards, and customer service. Is this what you mean?

Sujansky

Absolutely, and even sometimes it's more basic than that. Leaders may need to say things like, "This facility will stay open, but it will only be open for the next year," or "Your benefit package will not go away." It includes the higher-level things that you're talking about, but it's also some of these practical things. People think, "Oh, I'm going to get assigned to a new branch of the bank, and then I'm going to have to travel forty miles a day, not just ten." Or, "My schedule's going to change, and I took this job because the schedule works." So sometimes it's even more basic.

Wright

You've worked with corporate leaders for thirty years. What other recommendations do you have for them?

Sujansky

Well, I have one that's very real to me right now. I've been working on a small, pocket-sized book that's now in print, *The Keys to Motivating and Retaining Talent.* I happen to believe that this is a continual issue for corporations. When the economy is bad, sometimes our corporate leaders aren't as worried as they need to be about recruiting and retaining talent. It's not just about putting a person in a job. First, it is recruiting the real superstars, attracting people based on how your organization is unique. Then you need to figure out who the keepers are. I don't want to keep everybody I've ever hired, David, and I'll bet you don't either. So figure out who the keepers are. Then, when you know who they are (and I hope it's everybody you hire, but usually it isn't), recognize that certain jobs are harder to replace. Certain jobs are more expensive to replace. We know that either by their talent or a combination of their talent and the job they hold, we want to keep certain people.

Then we need to focus on things like balance of work and life, challenging work, and training and development opportunities. It's very interesting how very important training and development are to some people. I don't say this because that was my original profession. When people believe that they've entered a company where they won't remain marketable and they won't continue to learn, they leave. It's not just the money and the benefits that will keep them. They want to be coached. They want to have good leaders. Real key talent will sometimes say, "The leaders in this organization weren't doing what was needed strategically." So I think leaders need to figure out who the keepers are and recognize that the whole idea of recruiting and retaining remains a major issue. A recommendation I would have to a leader would be to put together a recruitment and retention policy. Make sure all of your key people know what it is. Pay attention to it. Make it a way of life, and work it.

Another thing I believe is that, as leaders, we really have to behave like we want our people to behave. I did a keynote yesterday about conquering change. In that keynote I talked a lot about some of the things that I believe in. After the talk, one of the people from the audience came over to Sandy Brown, our office manager, and said, "I'll bet she lives this too." I do, because Sandy quickly gave some examples of why spending five years with us here at KEYGroup has been some of the best five years of her employment. I really think that we have to walk the talk. It's actually very easy for me to do. When I don't behave the way I want other people to behave, I don't sleep and I don't feel well, so it must be ingrained in me. That's why I do this work. It's really the work I love. I think leaders need to model what they want. They need to treat the human resource as their most valuable asset. We've heard that for years and years, but I don't think we always see it being carried out. Pay attention to your talent and behave in a way that you keep them.

Wright

Joanne, I read your article in the *Pittsburgh Post-Gazette* and was fascinated by your research into the X and Y generations. Could you define the ages of the two generations and tell us a little about their differences?

Sujansky

It's interesting that you asked me to define the ages, because I think no one can really get that straight. You'll find for Gen X that some people say they were born in the early '60s to the mid-'70s, which I'm going to support for the purposes of this interview. There's a bit of dispute about where it starts and where it ends. Gen Ys are, for the most part, just entering the workforce, having been born in the late '70s to 1994. If you look at Gen X as having been in the workplace for a little while and Gen Y as still entering the workplace, it's probably the best way to estimate the age, at least for the purposes of this interview.

In terms of differences, let me talk about what I've experienced from some of our interns as well as individuals in some of the corporations in which I've worked. Gen Y, the younger ones, are really multitaskers. They are able to do more than one thing at once very easily. They are also extremely connected via the Internet and via e-mail. That's how they experience life. Everything has really been instant for them, and a lot of people talk about their having a sense of entitlement and expecting a lot of good things to happen to them. The mundane things bore them. As they enter the workplace, they want to be wired well. They don't want to wait for resources, because they're not used to waiting for things. They have access to information. Often they run circles around their bosses when it comes to being computer savvy.

I had one young man from the University of Pittsburgh, and I used to stand behind him while he was on the computer and say, "Wow! I didn't know it could do that!" It was incredible, and we've all been pretty well trained here. I think the difference with Ys is that they have been very connected to the electronic world from the time they were kids, and they are very much multitask-oriented. We also see a lot of social consciousness from that group. They're the Boomers' children. My three kids range in age from 10 to 22, and they're all Gen Y by the way we define this. Of course, within those three kids I see individual differences, and I see things that don't fit the so-called stereotypes either.

There are some things that are similar for the generations, but there are differences. For example, I'm a Boomer, but I am the oldest child. I am also a Boomer who came from a family with very little money. So some of my traits as a Boomer are different from what they describe as typical Boomer traits. I think it's important to understand that Generations X and Y will differ, but there will also be some similarities. Just as you look in the workplace and say this is a Boomer age, you might see a Boomer having more similar characteristics to Gen Ys. It could happen. Gen Xs were the first latchkey kids, so we saw a very high need for independence within that group. They really see their career path as a couple of years here and a couple of years there. They're pretty entrepreneurial in their outlook. Do you remember the term *intrapreneurial*, which means to be entrepreneurs inside a company? That's how I see Gen X. But I'll tell you something: I love a workplace with high diversity. I like a workplace with people a lot smarter than I am. I love that my most senior person involved with the business is in his sixties, and we have a 16-year-old artist and a 15-year-old student who helps us assemble gift packages for keynotes. In very large corporations it's hard for people to manage the generation mix. But this is just one type of diversity. It's a handful, but I think Gen X and Gen Y bring wonderful things to the workplace.

Some of the more senior leaders need help in understanding these generations. They misinterpret the motivations of Gen Y. Because Gen Ys are bored with the mundane, leaders often think they don't want to work. They misinterpret the impatience of Gen X. The ones I've experienced are not looking to climb the traditional ladder in the workplace, because they're thinking, "Within a couple of years I'll be somewhere else." The things that used to motivate the Boomers may not be same things needed to motivate Generation X. I challenge leaders to pay attention to different motivations in the workplace and to adjust accordingly.

Wright

I have a 40-year-old daughter and a 14-year-old daughter. I thought the reading skills of my youngest would be hurt by all this computerization. She is multitasking on the computer constantly, but she's reading at a college sophomore level even though she's only in eighth grade. It doesn't follow that if you multitask well or if you are a computer whiz that your basic skills will be anything other than enhanced, does it?

Sujansky

I think that there's probably a lot of evidence that your younger one was getting good life experiences in addition to her computer skills. I think the connectivity that we're talking about and the access to information enhance our lives. I think that, on the flip side, we need to remember that there are other ways to experience life, and that's important too. And, by the way, that 40-to-14 is a bigger gap than I have! If your 14-year-old is doing that well, other things have happened besides being so well connected.

Wright

You say that Generation X experienced a bleak job market, while Generation Y has experienced an economic expansion. How do their different experiences affect us now?

Sujansky

I think that we have to be prepared for an ever-changing marketplace. We should be coaching high school and college students on how to apply that diploma, degree, or those first few years of experience in multiple ways. We have several large healthcare organizations here in Pittsburgh as our clients. People are afraid to do elective surgery right now because there are not enough nurses, and they know it. We had the dot-coms making millionaires out of our Gen Xers. Maybe they've saved their money and at least the financial part of their lives is okay, but now they're looking for work. I think the message is that whatever we experienced upon entry into the workplace has probably already changed. In our lifetime we're probably not just going to have four or five jobs; we're probably going to have several careers. The safest way to think as managers and leaders is that Gen X, Gen Y, and the Boomers who are still in the workplace want to be marketable. They're entrusting their organizations to continually develop talent, because we will just continue to see the flux in the workplace.

Wright

Joanne, with our *Mission Possible!* talk show and book, we're trying to encourage people in our audience to be better, to live better, and to be more fulfilled by listening to the examples of our guests. Is there anyone or anything in your life that has made a difference for you and helped you to be a better person?

Sujansky

Maybe I'll approach that with both the "anything" and the "anyone" in mind. The "anything" for me would be that I'm the oldest of five children. My father was a mill worker and often subjected to strikes and layoffs, depending on what was going on with his employer at the time. I was responsible for a lot at a very early age and money was scarce. We had to be creative about how we had fun and what we did. I think that the early need to be responsible for myself and to help with the care of a handful of other kids at a young age had a huge impact on me. Most of it was good. I was independent and I matured early. I wanted to see the world, and that's why I've done so much traveling, because it was hard to get out of Freedom, Pennsylvania, to anywhere that cost more than a quarter on the bus. But I think that had a good impact. There were also probably some things about that experience that were tough. Sometimes I look back and wish that I had more playful times or more time to be a kid. In the end, my early responsibilities contributed to my ability to work hard and pay attention to people who have less than I do.

In terms of people who have made a difference for me, I think of two. My mother is 78 and the only grandparent remaining for my children. My mother loves unconditionally. She came to my talk yesterday because it was in her hometown. She brought twenty-three other relatives as well! She loves all five of us and our spouses equally. She adores her ten grandchildren. I watch her and I think, for me, the impact of her unconditional love has been very helpful and very strengthening.

The other person would be my husband. He is my opposite; therefore, since I am very right-brained, he helps me to develop my left brain. When I met him, I saw a calm and highly assertive individual. I'm from a family that readily shows a high level of emotion, so he brought a calm into my life. There are some messages that he sends to me continually that are very helpful. For instance, he says, "Let it go, honey. It's just not that big of a deal; let it go." This is when I'm mulling something over at two o'clock in the morning. There are little things too. I have no sense of direction, and he does. He has developed a side of me, as I believe I have done for him. We celebrated our twenty-fifth wedding anniversary this year. A lot of things and people have had an impact on me, especially in early life, but certainly these two people have helped me tremendously.

Wright

What an interesting conversation, and what a shame it's come to an end! You're such a nice and interesting person. I'd like to talk to you all day.

Sujansky

Thank you, David.

Wright

We have been talking to Dr. Joanne Sujansky. She is a Certified Speaking Professional. She owns her own business and speaks internationally, and she is a delight to talk to and is very intelligent. Thank you so much, Joanne, for being on *Mission Possible* today.

Sujansky

You're welcome, David. Thank you very much for having me.

About the Author

Dr. Joanne G. Sujansky, international speaker, author, and consultant, helps leaders to increase productivity and inspire loyalty. She is the owner of KEYGroup, a training and assessment firm. She is past National President of the American Society for Training and Development and is a recipient of their highest honor, the Gordon M. Bliss Award.

Joanne G. Sujansky, Ph.D., CSP
(Certified Speaking Professional)
1800 Sainte Claire Plaza
1121 Boyce Road
Pittsburgh, PA 15241-3918
(724) 942-7900
Fax: (724) 942-4648
E-mail: joanne@keypotential.com
www.keypotential.com

Chapter Eight – Dr. Joan Cassidy

-

David Wright (Wright)

Today we are talking to Dr. Joan Cassidy, founder and president of Integrated Leadership Concepts, Inc. (ILC). She is an internationally renowned quality management consultant, executive, coach, professor, speaker, and author. In addition to her consulting expertise, she is recognized as a dynamic motivational speaker and is often sought to address local, state, national, and international events on a wide variety of topics. She also is an adjunct professor for several Washington, D.C., area universities. Dr. Cassidy has published several books and numerous articles on quality and productivity improvement, creativity, performance improvement, communication, leadership, and other management topics. She has appeared on CNNfn, as well as a number of television and radio shows. In addition, she has hosted two business-oriented cable TV shows. Dr. Cassidy also is fluent in French and Spanish and has some capability in Russian, Italian, and German.

Dr. Cassidy, welcome to *Mission Possible!*

Dr. Joan Cassidy (Cassidy)

Thank you, David; I'm delighted to be here.

Wright

Dr. Cassidy, listed among your most requested topics is "whole-brain thinking." Could you tell our audience and readers what you mean?

Cassidy

Sure, I'd be glad to. Whole-brain thinking is my passion as far as my work is concerned. The concept of whole-brain thinking was made popular by Ned Herrmann. Ned used the research originally conducted by Roger Sperry. For those of you who don't know who he is, he won the Nobel Prize for his split-brain research during the 1970s. Up until that time we didn't have a good understanding of how the brain really worked. What Sperry found in his research has had a tremendous impact. For example, the left side of the brain is primarily responsible for logical, analytical, and sequential operations, whereas the right side is more holistic, spatial, and creative. When Ned happened upon this research, he got very curious about it. In fact, he was working for GE and was trying to develop a way to understand creativity better. He began developing his Herrmann Brain Dominance Instrument (HBDI) to measure the left/right brain dominance preferences originally identified in the Sperry research. However, Ned's research didn't demonstrate the left-right dichotomy, rather, it fell into four distinct categories—Upper Left/Lower Left and Upper Right/Lower Right. From there he developed his metaphorical model to explain people's preferences for how they communicate and how they think and solve problems. Whole-brain thinking means you access and use all four quadrants.

Wright

Let's see if I understand you. The brain has two halves, the right and left, and within these there are four quadrants?

Cassidy

Well, let me explain. When I do this, a lot of my audiences get confused and they think that I'm saying the brain is divided into four parts. That's really not the way it is. The original research showed that we basically use the left side of our brain for certain functions (analytical, sequential, logical) and the right side for others (spatial, creative, holistic). That notion still holds true, more or less. However, as I mentioned earlier, Ned's metaphorical model shows that people basically have preferences in four different categories: Upper Left, Lower Left, Upper Right, and Lower Right.

I use the following designations to describe these categories: "Analytical" (Upper Left), "Organizer" (Lower Left), "Experimental" (Upper Right), and "Interpersonal" (Lower Right). Analyticals prefer to use an analytical, logical, fact-based approach for thinking, communicating, and solving problems. They tend to focus on the bottom line. They're usually interested in technical and financial things. They develop strategic plans, goals, and objectives and care about efficiency. These types are the "thinker-uppers" and are usually found in the top echelons of an organization.

Organizers, on the other hand, even though they're also left-brain thinkers, live in the real world rather than an abstract world. They like to engage in hands-on activities. They are, for the most part, the backbone of any organization. You find lots of these types in organizations. They prefer to leave the "thinking up" to others (like the Analyticals) because they're the implementers. They prefer things that are organized, detailed, and chronological. They're very control-oriented. In other words, they don't like change. They like things to be in nice, tidy little boxes. This can create problems when you're trying to implement change.

The Upper Right Experimental types are conceptual, big-picture thinkers. They tend to be very intuitive and future-oriented. Their bent in life is inventing new solutions. They thrive on ambiguity and love looking at different ideas and pulling them all together to see how they connect. They solve problems intuitively rather than with the step-by-step approach used by the left-brain types. For example, think about math, in particular, algebra and geometry. Algebra is a left-brain, step-by-step mathematical concept. It is preferred by Analyticals. On the other hand, Experimentals prefer geometry because it's a spatial kind of math.

The fourth quadrant, the Lower Right, preferences are Interpersonals. These types prefer a people-impact perspective. They tend to be concerned about the "care and feeding" of the organization. One of their greatest strengths is working in teams. In fact, some people who are very strong Interpersonals don't function well unless they get feedback or are able to work in a relational mode. They make good teachers and facilitators. They generally focus on creating win-win situations. They want everybody to win. They don't like lose-lose. They're usually good in a customer service role.

In our western culture, especially in the United States, most of our organizations in the past have tended to be very left-brain oriented. As a result, many employees, especially Experimentals and Interpersonals, leave because they find this type of environment too confining. This really hurts the organization, particularly if the left-brainers are allowed to dominate. If this continues, the organization becomes stagnant without the creative types. And, without the interpersonal focus, employee morale tends to plummet and customer satisfaction declines.

Wright

As you were talking and explaining it to me, I seem to see some outgrowth into personality profiling. I'm familiar with the Myers-Briggs and also the DISC. Is the study of one a manifestation of the other?

Cassidy

The Myers-Briggs Type Indicator (MBTI) is based on Jungian psychology. In essence, the Myers-Briggs team observed and categorized behaviors and ultimately came up with their instrument. The Herrmann Brain Dominance Instrument (HBDI) has been highly correlated with the MBTI in a number of studies. Take, for example, the Myers-Briggs N/S (iNtuitive/Sensing) dimension. The N, or iNtuitive dimension, is correlated with the Upper Left (Analytical) and Upper Right (Experimental) quadrants. The S, or Sensing dimension, is correlated with the Lower Left (Organizer) and Lower Right (Interpersonal) quadrants. For the T/F (Thinking/Feeling) dimension, the T is correlated to the two left-brain quadrants, while the F is associated with the two right-brain quadrants. Finally, there is the J/P (Judging/Perceiving) dimension. The J is left and the P is right. When I have people compare their Myers-Briggs results to their Herrmann Brain Dominance preferences, there consistently is a fairly strong correlation. The only dimension where there is no correlation is the E/I—the Extrovert/Introvert dimension. And we are not really sure why that is so.

Wright

When you consider all the problems that people in the corporate world deal with, what stands out in your mind as the most difficult?

Cassidy

That's easy. There are two primary things. First, I consistently find that no matter what an organization calls me in to do, their primary issues usually boil down to *communication*—whether it is a matter of over, under, not enough of, or just basic misunderstanding. I believe one of the reasons we have these communication issues is because people in the organization don't understand the different ways people communicate based on the brain dominance preference. There are major differences.

Then there is the whole concept of *change*. Many organizations are going through a significant amount of change lately. And, for the most part, their efforts fail. One of the reasons they fail is because they don't understand the whole nature of change and the related consequences. Change is difficult. Change is slow. Too much change too fast is going to cause an initiative to fail. Furthermore, many people (especially the Lower Left Organizers) tend to resist change anyway. Then, circumstances are worsened because even those who are predisposed to accept the change may shut down if too much change is expected of them in a short period of time. So it's very important to understand that different people are going to respond to change differently. To be successful, you need to know what motivates different types. The "one-size-fits-all" concept doesn't work!

Wright

As a general rule, is there much difference in the methods and techniques used in motivating employees versus motivating volunteers?

Cassidy

For the most part, I find that it's essentially the same. In the first place, you really can't motivate anybody. The best you can do is to create an environment that is conducive to achieving goals and objectives, i.e., getting things done. If you're going to create that environment, you have to understand—and again I go back to my whole-brain thinking—*people are different.* We've learned from experience that what is one person's turn-on is another one's turnoff. If you know anything about expectancy theory and motivation, it says that when given choices people will choose what promises to give them the most reward or, to put it another way, they will choose what they value most. If you want people to be motivated, you've got to give them a reason. They have to see "what's in it for me." To achieve this, you have to build commitment.

You have to be clear in communicating wants, needs, and expectations. You have to make it exciting and valuable. At the same time, it has to be doable. If the standards are set too high, people basically give up and they just won't continue. You've got to give feedback, timely feedback, on what they're doing well and what needs to be changed. And then, of course, you have to reward successful performance. And again, keep in mind that what's important or valuable to me may not be to you.

The main distinction, I guess, in terms of employees versus volunteers is the whole notion of rewarding successful performance or holding people accountable. In a paid work environment, we can establish mechanisms to hold people accountable. Then they either do the work the way you want, or they don't get a paycheck and, ultimately, don't have a job, whereas in a volunteer organization you don't have that kind of a carrot or threat, depending on whichever way you want to look at it. Thus, it is even more difficult to keep volunteers motivated to continue. You have to make sure that people perceive a personal value in what they are doing. You've got to create that context or environment, whatever it is.

Wright

Most of us realize that in many companies teamwork is important. Building teams, however, is another story. With so many personality styles, how do you go about building teams?

Cassidy

That's a good one. One organization right now that I'm working with wanted me to do some team building and conflict management training. When I had my initial contact with them, the management painted the worst possible scenario in terms of what was going on. First, they said they've had a major change in their organizational mission. Next, they said that many of their employees have been there for twenty-plus years, and they just don't want to change. So there's a lot of finger pointing and, in some cases, dysfunctional behavior. I started out by introducing them to the whole-brain concept. It's amazing what we've accomplished in just a couple of different sessions. The director recently said, "I can't believe what you've done. They are actually working together better now!"

Diversity, especially when it comes to personality styles, is really a good thing; it's not a bad thing. Research shows that diverse thinking styles that are managed well consistently produce the best results. What makes it difficult is that most people don't understand that people have different styles. If they don't understand the theory and they don't know how to manage it, then they don't know how to manage the predictable conflict.

Wright

While reading an overview of your company, I read that one of your greatest strengths lies in the fact that you do not adhere to any one school or methodology; rather, you use an eclectic approach to training employees. Will you explain what you mean?

Cassidy

Sure. I guess first of all I have to go back about thirty years. During one of my earlier careers, I was head of the high school modern language department in Key West. I noticed that my students learned in different ways and that they didn't learn at the same rate. I had three classes of French 101 and two classes of Spanish 101. In each class, one group of students would be way ahead of the others, while another would be way behind. I thought that was kind of interesting. At the same time, I wanted to understand why this was happening. I said to myself, My primary goal is to make sure each student goes as far as they are capable of going and learns as much as possible. If they don't learn, it has to be at least partially my fault because I'm not the right kind of teacher for them.

In other words, I had to create the right environment for each of them. At the time, I hadn't heard of brain dominance or personality theories. This was during the early seventies. I only had my undergraduate degree, in French and Spanish with a minor in Russian. On the other hand, I am extremely intuitive and creative, so I started designing what I now understand to be whole-brain learning experiences. I started pulling from multiple sources in order to do so. I incorporated audio and visual elements. I also incorporated individual and small group activities. Each student was able to find something that they were good at. This helped them develop more confidence. As they developed confidence, they were able to function better in other activities. In a very short period of time I got national recognition for my innovative approaches. Some of my students, after only one year of taking a foreign language with me, would go off to college, pass their language entrance exam requirements and be able to take advanced placement. This was unheard of!

About a decade later, I changed careers and got involved in quality. I was totally fascinated by the fact that there were three primary quality gurus: Dr. W. Edwards Deming, Dr. Joseph Juran, and Phil Crosby. The interesting thing was, while each one was successful, they focused on different things. For example, Dr. Deming was the most whole-brained. He was analytical, but he also was the most right-brained with his focus on employee participation and involvement. Dr. Juran, on the other hand, focused on management activities and was very analytical. Finally, there was Phil Crosby, who seemed to focus on the Lower Left and Lower Right activities. Some people would swear by Dr. Deming. Others didn't like Deming but liked Juran, and still others opted for Crosby. All the while I kept saying there's good in each of them. You have to take what makes the most sense for each different situation.

When I finally went out on my own and started my own company, I chose the name Integrated Leadership Concepts. I thought about it for a long time, because I was concerned about what I saw everywhere—this compartmentalization. Leadership requires a "big picture" approach. In order to see the big picture you have to integrate different types of concepts and connect the dots. It's always been natural for me to do this because of my own preferences and style.

Wright

Dr. Cassidy, could you explain the difference between awareness, training, and education?

Cassidy

Sure. This is one of my pet peeves. I have a master's degree in curriculum design and a doctorate in adult education and human resource and organizational development. I've seen so much "stuff" that is being delivered as training, when in reality, it's not training! Organizations in the United States spend billions of dollars every year, yet training continues to get a bad rap because of the perception of little to no ROI (return on investment). I learned many years ago to make a distinction when it comes to awareness, training, and education.

Awareness is broad in nature. Information is delivered in a group context. Your purpose is to make individuals aware of a concept, or to provide them with resources on where to go to find additional information. There is little interaction. There is no attempt to see the extent to which individuals have acquired or enhanced a specific skill or skill set. I also refer to this as the "Talking Head" syndrome.

Training, on the other hand, is specific. It has a narrowly defined focus with clear objectives for what the individual is expected to do after completion of the training. And, probably the most important component, it has some feedback mechanism (observation or testing in some format) to determine if the individual can indeed perform the skill(s).

Finally, education takes training to a different level. For example, you learn how to do keyboarding (a skill formerly known as "typing") in order to operate a computer. Once you've learned that basic skill (how to keyboard), you learn how to apply it in a number of different contexts, e.g., word processing, spreadsheets, graphics and so forth. That is the major distinction.

With a concept like Effective Communication, you can deliver the basics during training, but then you have to provide additional opportunities for individuals to learn how to apply what they have learned in other contexts. Here's a good example: "If you give a man a fish you feed him for a day; if you teach him how to fish you feed him for a lifetime." I use this statement to describe the training/education differences. If I train him, I've fed him for the day. But if I educate him, then I've really provided him with that bridge to apply what he learned in other contexts.

Wright

With our *Mission Possible!* talk show and book, we are trying to encourage people in our audience to be better, live better and be more fulfilled by listening to the examples of our guests. Is there anything or anyone in your life that has made a difference for you and helped you to become a better person?

Cassidy

Oh, yes, there are several. Many, many years ago, when I was a high school student, I had a math teacher whom I initially was terrified of. I later found out that he was one of the most caring, considerate individuals that I have ever met. This man became my first mentor. He had a passion for teaching. I saw that passion and I guess it rubbed off on me. He also had a delightful sense of humor. He could be tough as nails, but he knew when to be tough and when to be soft or caring. I have tried to emulate him since then.

Also, the Myers-Briggs Type Indicator (MBTI) and later the Herrmann Brain Dominance Instrument (HBDI) had a tremendous impact on me. When I first completed the MBIT in 1979, I felt validated for the first time. As I result, I was motivated to make a career change. Up until that point in time I had done everything everybody told me to do. For example, I got a degree in foreign languages because my Spanish teacher said I was good in languages. In reality, I was more interested in psychology and management. The results of my MBTI gave me the impetus to make a career change. I got my doctorate and, in the process, became exposed to the Herrmann Brain Dominance Instrument. It was like a double WOW! Whole-brain thinking has been a catalyst to help me not only develop my own style, to understand why I do what I do, but also to help others.

Finally, the last thing that I want to mention is I've been single for more than thirty years. I was getting ready to go to my fortieth high school reunion. A former classmate saw my name and contacted me. To make a long story short, I found out he lived in Maryland, not too far from me. We got together, ended up dating, went to the reunion together, and he has been with me ever since. Jim is my soul mate, my companion, my best friend, my compass, and my strongest supporter!

Wright
That's a romantic story.

Cassidy
It really is. There's a whole lot more to it, but time is short!

Wright
Most people are fascinated with the new TV shows about being a survivor. What has been the greatest comeback you have made from adversity in your career or life?

Cassidy
There really hasn't been a single one, but a series. For example, I've been through two marriages and two divorces from two alcoholics. As a single parent, I raised two children, put both of them through college, and got three degrees myself—all on my own. I'm definitely a survivor!

Then last year I made the decision to move from Springfield, Virginia, to Odenton, Maryland, where I'm currently living. One of the primary reasons was to be with Jim. I also wanted to be closer to a long-term client. Finally, I wanted to leave the hectic pace and horrendous congestion in what is known as the "mixing bowl" in Springfield. I hadn't finished unpacking everything before our 9/11 tragedy occurred. As a result of that, one day I was making six figures plus and the next day I had no work. My long-term client had to lay off half of their workforce and subsequently end my contract. I had several speaking engagements that got cancelled. In fact, one of them was scheduled for September 11 and 12. Also, I was just about to sign another contract with a very prestigious company. Poof! Everything went up in smoke.

And, if that wasn't enough, I lost quite a bit of my retirement savings, which was in mutual funds. I went months and months with no work, no income, nothing. I initially panicked, worried about what I was going to do. But then I said to myself, Wait a minute. You've really got a lot to be thankful for. You're a lot better off than most people. Then I started looking at the pluses. I took stock of my skills and all the different things that I could do. I put my nose to the grindstone. I joined my Chamber of Commerce. Then I called everybody I knew. I sent out marketing materials. Within a couple months I began getting leads and referrals. Eventually, I got several adjunct teaching positions, and in the last couple of months I've had my hands full with almost more work than I can handle. It's just a matter of having that resolve and not giving up hope. And being thankful for what I've got.

Wright

If you could have a platform and tell our audience something you believe would help or encourage them, what would you say?

Cassidy

The first thing I would say is *know yourself.* I believe self-knowledge is the first criteria for success. The next thing I would say is *accept yourself.* You'll do better if you focus on your strengths rather than on your weaknesses. Once you've done that, you need to *develop a support system.* Identify people who are going to help you, not people who drag you down. Finally, I would say *develop a plan*—implement it, assess it, and make corrections as you go. Don't give up.

To wrap up: In the early eighties I was trying to figure out what I wanted to do. I met this very wise person whom I respected a great deal. I explained to him what I was doing and asked for his help. He said to me, "Here's what you've got to do. I call them the 'four gets': First, you *get knowledge,* then you *get good,* then you *get noticed,* and finally, you *get going*!" I've never forgotten that advice. God bless him, he's no longer with us. Every now and then I look back and think, Get knowledge—okay, got the additional degree. Get good—continue to hone my skills. Get noticed—do all the things I'm doing, like joining and being active in professional organizations, publishing books and articles, being interviewed on the TV and radio. And of course, get going—take action. Do something over which you have some control; don't fret about things over which you have little or no control. Stay positive!

Wright

We are down to the bottom of our half hour; time flies when you're having fun. Today we have been talking to Dr. Joan Cassidy. She is the founder and president of Integrated Leadership Concepts. She is an internationally known speaker, Certified Management Consultant, professor, coach, and author. We certainly have enjoyed visiting with her.

Thank you so much, Dr. Cassidy, for being with us on *Mission Possible!* today.

Cassidy
Thank you so much, David.

About the Author

Organizations that want results call Dr. Joan E. Cassidy, "The Organizational Doctor." For over twenty-five years, Fortune 100 and 500 companies and other private, public, and nonprofit organizations have dramatically increased productivity, consistently improved quality, and achieved unparalleled customer satisfaction after using her unique "whole-brain" model. She is a Certified Management Consultant, dynamic speaker, author, and professor.

Dr. Joan E. Cassidy, CMC
President, Integrated Leadership Concepts, Inc.
901 Nanticoke Run Way
Odenton, MD 21113
(410) 672-5467
Fax: (410) 695-2849
E-mail: DrJoanC@aol.com
www.DrJoanCassidy.com

Chapter Nine – Lisa Newman Bevington

-

David Wright (Wright)

Today we are talking to Lisa Newman Bevington, who is the executive director and owner of Health Management Partners, Inc., a provider of employee assistance programs (EAPs), consulting and training. Ms. Bevington has a master's degree in business administration and is both a Senior Professional in Human Resources (SPHR) and a Certified Employee Assistance Professional (CEAP). Ms. Bevington has been a member of the board of directors of the Employee Assistance Society of North America (EASNA) and a member of the faculty at Tulane University and the University of New Orleans, where she has taught human resource management courses and professional development training programs. She was one of the founding board members of the Louisiana Managed Healthcare Association. In 1991, Ms. Bevington received an award for teaching excellence from Tulane University, and in 1993 she was recognized as one of eight Achievers by the Women Business Owners Association of New Orleans. Prior to founding Health Management Partners, Ms. Bevington held positions in banking and management consulting.

Lisa Bevington, welcome to *Mission Possible!*

Lisa Newman Bevington (Bevington)

And welcome to you!

Wright

Lisa, your past career experience is very impressive. You have worked for large, well-respected companies in the financial industry. What led you to change careers to the health management industry?

Bevington

I really work in a side of health management known as employee assistance. Early in my career I worked for a very large bank, and I also worked for a smaller bank. I worked for a large accounting firm and then a major corporation and finally a large consulting firm. Those were great experiences, and they taught me a lot; but throughout that time I knew there was something, some element, that was below or beneath the financial numbers that was affecting productivity. To me, that element was the emotional and psychological well-being of the employees. Employees are human beings. They're not robots, although the companies I've worked with do have robotic technology! But employees are human beings—they come to work and bring their personal lives into the workplace. They can't just hang them up at the door with the coat or put them on the rack when they put on their uniform. I felt that sometimes when we were doing our budgeting or human resources analyses, we were missing something that affected productivity.

Wright

Lisa, I know that through your company you assist corporations in managing troubled employees. What I'm not sure about is how you define a troubled employee.

Bevington

We define a troubled employee as anyone who has something else going on in their life that's keeping their mind off of their job. That could be a sick child. It could be as simple as not getting sleep at night because the baby was up crying. It could be a marriage that's falling apart or a fight you had with your spouse. It could be an addiction problem or a chronic depression. But it doesn't have to be a diagnosable mental illness. Sometimes when we talk to employers about our services they say, "If anybody was crazy around here, we would know it." We're not necessarily talking about somebody whose elevator doesn't go to the top. I ask this at every training and every speech I make: "Who can honestly raise their hand and say they have never gone to work with something else going on in their mind that interferes with keeping their mind on their job that day?" That's your troubled employee. That troubled employee affects not only your productivity but your safety and morale—whether it's adding extra zeros to wire transfers or forgetting to do a task that's important. In a safety-sensitive environment, one second of thought away from what you're doing could cause a very serious accident. That's the troubled employee. And the new frontier of safety is not the rickety ladder or the unsafe condition. It's the unsafe act by the employee that for one split second doesn't have their mind on what they're doing. It's the unsafe act, not the unsafe condition.

Wright

After you work with a corporation, do you ever get directly involved with any of your clients' employees?

Bevington

Most of the direct work with the employees is done by others. Mostly I consult with management about the human resource policies, about strategies, procedures, and techniques. Occasionally I do speak directly with an employee when my expertise is appropriate to their concern. Our services cover such workplace issues as sexual harassment, for instance. When someone calls into our service and says that they're being harassed on the job, then certainly they're going to get a call back from me or another workplace expert who's going to start asking some questions: "What kind of harassment? Who have you told this to? Let's talk about this a little further."

We also provide legal consultations, financial, child and elder care, as well as psychological help and assistance with addiction concerns. Anytime something might fall into the realm of my expertise, I might consult directly on a case. I work a lot with management of stalking cases, so I might talk to someone who's being stalked in the workplace or by a co-worker or vendor associated with the workplace who's stalking them outside of the workplace.

Wright

I had a family member who was an alcoholic and worked for many years with a large company that had federal contracts. They really couldn't straighten out the problem because he was a member of the union and the union kept fighting on his side, even when what he was doing was dangerous. Do you ever have any trouble with outside agencies or people like unions?

Bevington

Yes, we do. We sometimes have trouble with employers themselves not believing that what their own employee is doing is dangerous. Or they think it's not that bad, and they've told him to stop. Sometimes it's not taken very seriously.

Wright

While researching information for this interview, I was fascinated to learn of the financial as well as physical dangers inherent in having troubled employees, such as "workplace violence." Is that a real problem?

Bevington
It's a very, very real problem.

Wright
How does it manifest itself?

Bevington
Starting at the top, workplace homicide is the third leading cause of death in the workplace. For many years it was the second leading cause of death in the workplace. Among women it's the number one leading cause of death in the workplace. A woman is more likely to die at work by being killed by someone else than any other way. It's the most dangerous activity in the workplace. Vehicular homicide is number one for men, so we all know that driving a car or truck is very dangerous. Outside of that, being murdered is one of the more dangerous things that can happen to you in the workplace.

I think this is very, very serious. We all have a right to come home from work. There's somewhere between seven hundred and a thousand homicides in American workplaces every year. That means in a decade far more people are killed in American workplaces than were killed in the World Trade Tower. I think this is very, very scary. That's just the tip of the iceberg. As many as one in five women will be stalked over their lifetime, as well as a significant number of men. Much of the stalking occurs in the workplace or relative to the workplace. Assaults and threats are very common. There are some estimates that as many as 100,000 people are harmed in the workplace and up to one million employees in America are victimized at work each year. When you think of it, at home we have dogs and alarm systems and we lock our doors. But at work anybody can walk in. They can walk in and attack you. You're working with dozens, if not hundreds, of strangers.

Statistics show that as many as one in five high school students, much less adults, and in some of the southern states as many as one in two, are armed on our bodies, in our purses, or in our cars. So you're dealing with someone you don't know very well; you don't know their past very well. They may well be armed, and you don't have your attack dog or personal alarm system there. Workplaces have got to wake up and take some safety precautions. Some of our recent cases have included two women getting into a fight and one bit the other one. We had one person threaten the other person, and the other person was known to carry a gun. We had a manager who carried a gun in his briefcase and left it open on his desk while he had talked to employees. I've managed a case of two doctors, one stalking the other one for a business deal that went wrong several decades ago. Other cases involved a boyfriend who came into one workplace, jumped over a security desk, and began strangling his estranged girlfriend; a fellow in the workplace who threatened to kill a vendor; and an employee who threatened to cut his supervisor into little bitty pieces. When I found out he was a woodworker who worked with chainsaws, I was a little bit concerned.

Domestic violence coming to work is a big concern. Most companies want to hide their heads in the sand. The events of 9/11 have opened some eyes, but just not enough. I can say, David, that for years I talked about the risk of school violence just as a public service. Whenever I did training or gave a talk about workplace violence, I told them to think about the school system. What's being done to protect your children at school? Go and ask some questions. We know that teenagers are armed. We know that teenagers will harm. Go and ask some questions about your school's policies. Now I don't have to say that anymore, and I think that's really, really sad. Now it's believable.

Wright
You talk about managing these kinds of problems. Why don't the bosses just fire them for things that go wrong? Where does the word *manage* come in?

Bevington
What you want to do is detect the subtle signs way in advance. Then you want to assess how serious the threat is, and you want to keep assessing that over time to see if that grows. By the time someone is actually threatening to harm or to kill someone, they should not be in your workplace. I'm a firm believer in that. I can tell you, I get far too many cases where the person has made multiple threats to kill people and may even have a list that they carry around with them of the people they want to kill, and they are still at work. Some of these are professional people.

Wright
So yours is preventative medicine more than anything else?

Bevington

Yes. We want preventative policies; but anytime somebody says something that could be construed in any way as violent or acts in any way in a violent manner, we want to address that instantly and assess it. If there's any written correspondence, we want to assess that. We want to nip it in the bud. We want to make sure there are policies and procedures to protect the workplace, that there's security in place, photographs of the employees so that if they're taken off-site somebody knows what they look like if they were to come back on-site. And there are ways to prevent them from coming back on-site. There are ways of making sure that information, these little subtle innuendoes, are passed up to human resources when they start happening and not later when the press says, "Tell us about this guy," and people say, "Oh, he's been saying things like this for years" . . . but nobody told anyone.

Wright

For years, I have concerned myself with co-worker conflicts, reduced interest or motivation, and lack of effective training. Are most companies aware of the tremendous risks involved if they do not consider risk management?

Bevington

Most companies want to stick their heads in the sand about this.

Wright

Is it because they don't want to get involved in personal lives?

Bevington

They just don't want to believe it could happen to them. Whether it's reduced motivation or fear, effective training is the key to success. The rapid changes in our society and in our workplaces have lead to such widespread anxiety, disloyalty, and fear. This has to be addressed for maximum productivity to be achieved. Long after 9/11 our phone lines are still full of callers who are living on the edge. Maybe they were already living on the edge, but now they're very, very afraid. They're afraid of losing their jobs. They've lost money, maybe in the stock market. They've seen their companies downsize. Maybe they're depressed or suicidal. These are the workers who have kept their jobs; these aren't the ones who have lost their jobs. We run an employee assistance program, and to call us you have to be an employee. So these are the people who still have their jobs. I think that training, motivational speaking, communication are key to success—having plans for risk assessment and what you're going to do when these things happen. I think some of these anthrax scares and terrorist activities opened up some eyes. It's so easy to say, "It wouldn't happen here." Well, it would happen here—maybe not exactly what happened at the World Trade Towers, but in small ways. I have probably ten active cases in New Orleans of people who've made threats to do something to one or more other people. That's just in one city, one business. I'm not the FBI or the CIA. I'm a private company, so I don't know about the terrorist activities. I only know about the employees that are threatening to do things to other employees in forty companies.

Wright

I remember telling you a few weeks ago that I had recently published a book on the subject of stalking, written by a lady in New York. While reading it, I found terror in both male and female stalking. I was really frightened.

Bevington

Absolutely; it's very scary. I think that it's very important to have these controls and policies in place ahead of time so you know what to do. We had a workplace here in New Orleans where a man killed his family—two children and his wife—and then turned himself in. There was some period of time where the workplace didn't know he had turned himself in to the police and they were very scared that he might then come there, because there have been many cases where people killed their family and then came to work and killed people. They were also so upset, wondering if they could have seen any sign of this. Then the media descended on them. This had never happened before. It's not something that you think is going to happen, so it's a very scary thing for them.

That's the kind of thing you have to think about, unfortunately, in these times. Once it happens you go a little nutty yourself. You're upset, so you're not making good decisions. It's the kind of thing you need to think about ahead of time, before you're upset, because you're part of the situation.

Wright

On a smaller scale I can understand how it would stop work. Our company's office is directly across the street from a magnificent, 200-year-old courthouse. My office has windows that look right out at it. Our whole staff looked out a few weeks ago and saw a lot of people milling around in the front yard of the courthouse. We thought there was a bomb scare, so everybody stopped working. Finally one of our employees walked across the street to find out what was wrong. They were having an auction! But the fear had stopped everything.

Let's change the subject for a minute. With our *Mission Possible!* talk show and book, we are trying to encourage people in our audience to be better, live better, and be more fulfilled by listening to the examples of our guests. Is there anything or anyone in your life that has made a difference for you and helped you to become a better person?

Bevington

Absolutely. I think the clients that I work with who overcome tremendous obstacles and tragedy inspire me every day. Anybody who thinks they're down and out just needs to come and work my phone lines for a few hours and they'll be inspired. The feedback we get saying "Thank you for being there" is not for me personally but for a team of counselors and other people, financial planners, whatever it takes. Some of them are sent to us because they failed drug tests and are about to lose their job. Their wife or husband may have already left them. When they overcome their addiction, when they bring their life up, let us know they're back, they've made it, they've dug themselves out of the hole, that is just so motivational to me! The organizations that hire me and trust me with some of their toughest situations of trying to prevent people from killing people, trying to prevent lawsuits, and trying to help people—that motivates me, as well as inspirational books and tapes and special people.

Just this weekend there was a series in our local newspaper about a young woman who died right before her high school graduation. She lived with cystic fibrosis and just made the most of her seventeen years. Her parents told her when she was young and crying about her condition, "You can be bitter or you can be better. We don't know how long you have to live, but this is your life. You can make something out of it or not." She decided to get every bit of good she could out of her life. Reading her story was such an inspiration to me that I read it twice.

Also, there's the love and support of my family; I have a large extended family—I started to say crazy!—and, of course, my faith in God. And I have to mention therapy. Therapy has helped me overcome some old behavior patterns and have the courage to see things in new ways. I think, most importantly, being around positive people like you, David, and people in your organization. The seminar I attended just a few weeks ago from your organization was great. I was on a high from that. I think all of these things are so important, and then being around positive and inspirational people.

Wright

Most people are fascinated with the new TV shows about being a survivor. What has been the greatest comeback you have made from adversity in your career or life?

Bevington

Almost seven years ago I nearly died. It turned out I had five or six bleeding ulcers that I didn't know about. I never had any stomach pain; I could eat gravel and Tabasco. I think surviving that and coming back from that was important. But I'd have to say my divorce maybe two years after that was my absolute lowest point.

At the same time as my divorce, my business was in a time of transition and there were a lot of decisions that had to be made. I had a business partner then, and she and I disagreed on which route to take the business. I ended up buying her out of the business during the middle of my divorce, which was really hard.

My young son was suffering from the marital strife and separation. I think one of my goals in life had always been to have a happy marriage. We had been married ten years. My son needed my time and my business needed my time. It just wasn't a good situation. I guess I survived by just taking it one day at a time—the AA motto. Every night I said thanks to God that I made it through the day, that I still had a roof over my head, hadn't declared bankruptcy, had paid my bills, had my health. I knew how important that was since I had nearly died a couple of years prior. At that time that was enough. I had to scale way back on what success meant to me.

Ultimately, I sacrificed a lot of business opportunities to focus attention on my son. I don't have any regrets about that. I could be way further ahead with my business if I hadn't done that, but I have a fantastic teenager now and we have a great relationship. There's no other measure of success, no amount of money or business success that could mean more to me than that. I feel proud of the decisions and sacrifices I had to make, and I still have a lot more years in me.

Wright

If you could have a platform and tell our audience something you believe would help or encourage them, what would you say?

Bevington

I'd say have faith in yourself. Faith is very important to me. The ultimate role in my life is my faith in God. You can meet your goals and fulfill your dreams despite what others may say. There are powerful negative influences out there every day telling me and telling you that you're not good enough, that you can't do this and you can't do that. Make sure you stay focused on the positive.

The other thing I've learned to do is to practice courage every day. I try to do some little thing I haven't done before that I've been scared to do. Yesterday—and I know this sounds silly—I picked up a cockroach. Now, he was dead and I used napkins, but I'd never picked up a dead cockroach before. That's what my man always used to do; but I'm a single woman, and there's no man that works in my business right now. We were having visitors, and there were a couple of cockroaches in the bathroom, so I put together some paper towels, got real brave, and reached down and picked up that cockroach and threw him in the trash. Then I ran out and took a poll. Only one of the women that I work with had ever picked up a cockroach, dead or alive, with a napkin, vacuum, or anything, so I felt really proud of myself. I know you, as a man, don't think that's a big deal!

Year before last I trailered a boat and backed it into the water. That's something else men have always done for me. I could just snap my finger and say, "Boys, I'd like to take a ride in the boat now."

Right now, outside, I'm building a swimming pool. I'm a single woman and I'm building a swimming pool. Everybody from my parents to the real estate agent have told me it's the stupidest thing in the world. I'm never going to get my money back; it's totally stupid. But I have always wanted a swimming pool, and the bank was fool enough to give me the money, so they're out there building my swimming pool.

Wright

The goal is not to make money; the goal is to swim. Don't they realize that?

Bevington

Well, I'm going to swim in it, and I'm going to swim in it quite a few thousand dollars' worth!

Wright

This has been an interesting conversation. We have been talking to Lisa Newman Bevington, the executive director and owner of Health Management Partners. She is an intelligent business lady and, as we have found out, a great mom.

We appreciate your participation, Lisa; thank you so much for being on *Mission Possible!* today.

Bevington

Thank you so much, David, for this opportunity.

About the Author

For over twenty years Lisa Newman Bevington has brought to the workplace her knowledge of how to increase productivity and profits through better management of troubled employees. As an Employee Assistance Program (EAP) provider, she has firsthand experience helping managers and employees implement cost-effective strategies that work. Her real-life messages are thought-provoking and entertaining.

Lisa Newman Bevington
P.O. Box 9070
Mandeville, LA 70470
(985) 624-4842
Fax: (985) 624-2622
E-mail: LisaB@ConsultHMP.com

-

Chapter Ten – Bruce Christopher

-

David E. Wright (Wright)

Today we're talking to Bruce Christopher, who is considered America's foremost "Enter-Trainer." He has earned this distinction because of his high-energy style and the humorous presentation of his material. He is a licensed psychologist, holding degrees in professional psychology as well as interpersonal communications. Bruce has captivated audiences internationally because of his humorous approach to today's topics that impact our personal and professional lives. His popular topic *Why Are Women So Strange and Men So Weird?* sells out to standing-room-only crowds at national conventions, corporate conferences, and sales meetings. Bruce is a credentialed professional speaker, a member of the international Who's Who of Entrepreneurs, National Speakers Association, Meeting Professionals International, and is a practicing supervising clinical psychologist.

Bruce Christopher, welcome to *Mission Possible!*

Bruce Christopher (Christopher)

Thank you so much; glad to be here.

Wright

Bruce, you have stated in your keynote addresses, as well as in your seminar *Why Are Women So Strange and Men So Weird?,* that men and women think, speak, and make decisions differently. Can you tell us a little bit about what you mean?

Christopher

I certainly can. As you can imagine, it's a very, very popular topic, and I do it a lot for many organizations and companies. Basically, what I try to bring out in my seminars is that sometimes men and women are on a bit of a different page of music in terms of how we think, how we speak, and how we make decisions. If we really don't know what that different page is, we're not going to be very effective, especially in terms of working with one another, in sales, and, of course, in managing people of the opposite sex. How men and women think differently seems to have some genetic underpinnings.

Men tend to think in what I call a *compartmental mode,* that is, they tend to put things into boxes in their head, and they tend to see the separateness between issues. Women are sort of the opposite. Women think in more of a *global format.* Where men see the separateness, women see the connectivity between issues and between things that are going on. This can create a lot of frustration.

In terms of how we speak differently, men tend to be a little bit more *bottom line-oriented.* They go over the details fairly quickly and don't want to spend time on the story or the historical narrative. Women tend to do the opposite. They tend to work up to the bottom line, spending a lot of time on the *details and the story.* These stylistic differences can then create frustration in our relationships. Women often perceive that men are tuning them out, and probably rightly so; because when men don't get that bottom line quickly enough, they tend to do that. On the other hand, women complain that men don't listen and that men interrupt them too much. Again, that's a formation of this different speaking style that we have.

The same holds true in terms of how we make decisions. Probably because men are very compartmental, we use a style of decision making that I call *product decision making.* It tends to be a unilateral type of decision-making mechanism. We tend to go right for the answer as fast as we can. That's what we want. Women, because they're more global-oriented, tend to use a style called *process decision making.* Women are more interested in the consensus of the decision, where everyone puts their two cents in, and we come to a hopefully unanimous decision together. There are strengths and weaknesses for all these different types. What I try to bring out in my seminar is that a fully functioning team, or relationship, for that matter, works best when we are able to bring out the strengths of both men and women.

Wright

Rather than just understanding the differences, would it not be good for both genders to learn from each other how to make decisions differently, how to speak and think differently?

Christopher

Absolutely. In fact, I really spend a lot of time on applications in my seminar. I really want to try to get men and women to be more bilingual. Whereas men speak *voice-male,* they need to learn to speak a little more *voice-female* to be more effective, and vice versa. I say things like this: Men need to spend more time on the details, not glossing over the process. Conversely, women need to get to the bottom line quicker. These are just simple strategies that we can employ to help us be more effective. I give the men about ten applications and the women about ten applications.

Wright

Have women in business, at least those who have attained leadership roles, learned the art of speaking as a man speaks? If not, maybe this is why, in many cases, men have so many problems working for women.

Christopher

That's a great question. I think that's true. I think women tend to be a little more flexible and innovative in their communication style—they've learned that over the years. Women in management have learned to adopt the male style of speaking because corporate America tends to be more compartmental and bottom line-oriented than it is global and detail-oriented. Women who are in management circles adopt that style, and it makes them successful too.

Wright

You have said that excellent communicators have better relationships at work and at home. Can you give our listeners and readers any tips on how to become better communicators?

Christopher

I think one of the greatest tips is to understand the difference between *understanding* and *agreement*. To be a great communicator, you have to have what's called *empathy*. That is the skill of connecting with the feelings of the speaker and then being able to reflect it back to them. Sometimes in a relationship people will say, "You're not listening to me," or "You're not hearing what I'm saying." What they really mean is, "You don't agree with me." The key to being a great communicator is being able to understand and connect with where someone is, but that doesn't necessarily mean you agree with him or her. For example, you may have a social issue that you really believe in, to which I may be diametrically opposed. If I'm a great listener, I'm going to be able to put myself in your shoes for a little bit and connect with your perspectives and your feelings and understand where you're coming from. That does not necessarily mean that I agree with you. If I'm going to be a great communicator, I then will reflect that back to you. I may say something like, "You believe in this issue because of your feelings about such and such and such, right?" You would say yes, and then you would know that I have connected with your perspective and feelings. A lot of people don't do that, because they think when they empathize with you and understand you, somehow they're giving up their own ground or conceding their own territory. But that's not the case at all. I think that's key in negotiation and in listening—to be able to understand the other party and not confuse that with agreement.

Wright

So if you say something like "I understand exactly what you're saying, and I can see how you feel that way," that would eliminate the you-don't-listen-to-me syndrome?

Christopher

Definitely. Again, in relationships people want their own way, so we become polarized and try to express what we want, but the other person may not agree with us. Then we'll say something like, "You're not listening to me," when in fact they may well have heard us and understood us. Many times in relationships we have to get to the point of the *art of disagreement,* and that disagreeing is okay.

Wright

I have heard for many years that people use the word *attitude* in many ways; obviously a good, positive attitude has proven to be better than a bad or negative attitude. In your program *Are We Having Fun Yet?* you say that attitude creates success. I've never heard someone use the word *create* before in that context. What do you mean?

Christopher

That program is a very humorous session on the difference between optimism and pessimism. There have actually been some studies done on those differences. There's a huge movement of study right now called *emotional intelligence.* Part of that is studying how our attitude, or what we bring to the table every day in terms of our attitude—whether we're an optimist or a pessimist—does create success. Basically, what the studies have indicated (and these are long-term studies) is that pessimists actually get sick more in life than optimistic people. Pessimists have worse relationships; they have a higher divorce rate. They're not as good parents as optimistic people. And pessimists actually make less money in life than optimistic people. There are several studies that I cite in my seminar that would demonstrate that. If you're a positive, optimistic person, you know how to deal with failures and challenges in an appropriate manner. You're probably going to be more successful in whatever field you choose, and you'll probably make more money.

Wright

I believe being a positive person and an optimistic person affects everything from mental health to physical health. I've noted that a lot of people who tend to be pessimists all the time don't actually understand that they're pessimists. If you ask them, they would say that they are optimists. Is that true?

Christopher

That's very true. In fact, one of the things I do in my seminars is have the audience take a test. Right away I'll say to the group, "How many people think that you're an optimistic person? Raise your hand." Ninety-nine percent of the people raise their hand. Then as we go through the seminar, I have them take a test on what optimism really is, and seventy percent of them fail it because they don't know what optimism really is all about. Most people think that optimism means being in a "zippity-do-dah, everything's great" mood, but optimism really has more to do with our response to challenges and failures and mistakes we make. It has nothing to do with luck or having things go our way. So you're right; most people are sort of blind to the fact that they're pessimists.

Wright

Let me quote you if you don't mind. You state, "Life is change. Growth is optional." Is it possible to change without growing?

Christopher

I don't think so. I think that change and growth come together, and they usually come together through the conduit of pain. Life, as we all know, has changed since 9/11, and the economy has taken a lot of hits. If there's one thing you can count on in life, it's that life is going to change on you. Life is going to throw you a curveball, and a lot of times you're not going to get what you expect. For a lot of us, our portfolios are really down right now, and we're not getting what we counted on. How are we going to deal with that? That's the big question. These changes are painful. I call these moments of change "catalyst events." As in chemistry, a catalyst is sort of a chemical kick in the rear to get a reaction going between two elements or two compounds. That's what we experience as adults. We have catalyst events that sort of kick us in the behind and get us going either in the direction of growth or in the direction of becoming stagnant. I don't think we can grow without change, without those catalyst events. Like working out or jogging, it's painful when we do it, but you cannot become physically healthy without that pain.

Wright
Without it, it would be impossible to test our mettle, would it not?

Christopher
Absolutely.

Wright
When you do training sessions and seminars for corporations, how do you teach them to keep up with change, especially when you consider downsizing, mergers, and technological advances?

Christopher
Here's an interesting story. I spoke two days after the 9/11 attack. The attack came on Tuesday and I spoke on Thursday. I use a lot of comedy and humor in my presentations, and, frankly, two days after the attack I didn't feel like being very funny. Oddly enough, the title of my presentation for this group was *Innovate or Stagnate*. It was on how to deal with change. One of the things I did was I got up in front of the audience, spoke a little bit, and then asked them to think about change differently. I pointed out that optimists know that within every negative event are the seeds of opportunity. I said, "Let's apply this to what happened two days ago." Of course, we were still grieving from that. I said, "What would be some of the good things that could come out of what happened two days ago?" We began to brainstorm as an audience, and in about five minutes we came up with thirty-eight potential good things that could come out of the tragedy of 9/11.

Wright
You're kidding.

Christopher

No, it was an amazing moment. What it did for us as an audience was teach us the number one skill of dealing with change, that is, to be able to see change as a seed for something that can grow, something positive and something opportunistic. There we were, experiencing it at this most horrendous time. I'll never forget that day.

Wright

All of us have trouble dealing with difficult customers, bosses, neighbors, coworkers, or even families. You have a program titled *Bambi Vs. Godzilla* that seems to address the problem. Could you give us some advice on handling difficult people?

Christopher

Sure. In this program I talk about six basic difficult personality types. Some of them might be *exploders*, people who blow up on you with anger. I also talk about *snipers*, people who use sarcastic humor to get you. Then, of course, there are the *know-it-alls*. (There are a lot of know-it-alls in corporate America.) Finally, we have the ever-present *whiners*, the people who are negative and complain about everything. What I help the audience to understand is that the first thing you have to know is that these people aren't evil. What they really have is defense mechanisms that they use to help get their way. An exploder explodes for a reason. He or she thinks that by blowing up they'll get the result they want. It's something that they've learned probably since childhood. I really help the audience to stop and not prejudge too much, then get underneath the behavior and look for the drivers of that behavior. I help the audience do that for every difficult personality type. If you can figure out what the driver is—why the exploder explodes, why the complainer complains—then you can formulate a real-time strategy to help them change their ways so they won't continue in their behavior, especially around you. That's the number one thing I try to get audiences to do—to get underneath the skin of other people and figure out what's driving their behavior.

Wright

I've been in sales all my life and love it. There was a man many years ago who made my life a lot easier when he taught me how to handle difficult, complaining people. Now when someone complains, I say, "Tell me all of it." I'll listen and say, "Oh my, that's terrible. Do you have any more?" I just let them dump it all. Pretty soon their bucket is empty. It sounds humorous, but it's helped me, because prior to that I was trying to stifle what they were saying, thinking that if they didn't say it, it didn't exist.

Christopher

That's a technique I call the "surprise effect." People like the complainer you were just talking about are used to complaining, and they're used to having people respond to them in a certain way—maybe even try to stifle them or talk them out of it by saying, "Oh, things aren't that bad." But the surprise effect, basically, is doing the exact opposite of what they expect you to do. Your technique of saying "Tell me more, get it all off your chest" surprises them. When you introduce that kind of surprise, it changes the outcome of the communication.

Wright

My wife is a cancer survivor, and a lot of times all I can do is sympathize with a cancer patient who is going through some horrible chemotherapy treatments or whatever. I've watched my wife several times, and it's almost a technique—although I'm sure she wouldn't call it that. When someone says something is bad, she will say, "It will probably get worse, but the good news is you're going to make it through." It's kind of the same thing.

Christopher

She sounds like an optimist.

Wright

She certainly is! Tell us a little bit about risk taking. I was interested in your program titled *Leap! The New Will Appear*. I love that title. It seems to help people crash through their comfort zones. Can you tell us how you make that come about?

Christopher

I've done this with small groups of twenty people, on up to four thousand people as well. I put the entire audience in a game situation, and I have two teams competing against one another. In order to win the game, you have to do certain things. One of the first things you have to learn to do is take a risk. To win the game, people have to put themselves on the line; they have to act in a way they're not used to or comfortable with, and they have to employ some creative problem solving. As they compete as a team, what magically happens is it creates this incredible bond and community within the team members. They learn the skills of communication and teamwork, also risk taking and creative problem solving. We usually play the game for about half an hour. It's pretty funny and people are laughing and hooting it up. After the game, I'll come back and outline the five essential ingredients for success that were used in order to win at the game. One of the main things that happens is that they really have to crash out of their comfort zone. I talk about the whole concept of comfort zones and why we're most comfortable when we are in the middle of them. One of the primary things I want them to understand is this: When you leap into your fear, your fear disappears. That's what they experience, because they're usually afraid to do this; but then when they do it, they realize it wasn't that bad, and, in fact, they feel a lot more energized and confident.

Wright

With our *Mission Possible!* talk show and book, we're trying to encourage people in our audience to be better, to live better, and to be more fulfilled by listening to the examples of our guests. Is there anyone or anything in your life that has made a difference for you and helped you to be a better person?

Christopher

When I think about that question, there's one guy that comes to my mind. This happened twenty years ago, when I was learning how to downhill ski. He was my best friend, Joe, a tremendous competitive skier. I had not skied a day in my life, so I asked him to teach me how to ski—I've remembered this for twenty years. He brought me to the mountain and I put on my skis. I said, "Okay, Joe, tell me what to do." I anticipated that he was going to give me a lot of technical or technique advice on how to stand, swivel, and all of that, but he only said one thing to me. His entire advice for that day was, "If you don't fall a lot today, you're not trying hard enough." And that's all he said. As I think back on that day, I remember I fell probably a hundred times. I remember one time I fell at the top of the hill and slid all the way down on my rear end, bowling into a line of people waiting for the chairlift. I heard people laughing at me as I was lying there, and I actually had the thought, "Wow, I must be trying really hard today." I've always remembered Joe's little statement as a lesson in life. If we don't fall down a lot, we're probably not trying hard enough. It's okay to fall down, and it's okay to make a mistake. Learn from it. I thank Joe for that; he had an impact on me.

Wright

What do you think makes up a great mentor? In other words, are there characteristics that mentors seem to have in common?

Christopher

I think of two things that a mentor has to have. One is a caring attitude. They need to be willing to give back. I've always said to myself that if I ever achieve what I want to achieve in my profession and career, I want to give back to young people or people who are just starting out. Mentors have to have that kind of caring, altruistic attitude.

The other thing is this: Mentors need to be on fire themselves. Someone once said to me that vision is not taught, it's caught. Mentors need to have a passion for what they're doing. They need to be excited about their career and their job in life. You can't really teach that; other people become infected by it when they're around you. Mentors need to have a little fire in the belly. They need to be passionate about what they're doing.

Wright

Most people are fascinated with these new television shows about being a survivor. What has been the greatest comeback that you have made from adversity in your career or in your life?

Christopher

That's a great question; there are many. A lot of speakers talk about how they overcame this or that, and then they build their career off of that one story. I've had some amazing things happen to me; I've been laid off from jobs that I thought I was going to be at forever. I've had cancer. Three years ago I was diagnosed with rheumatoid arthritis. I've gone through a lot of stuff, but I don't talk about those things in my programs, because I don't want to sensationalize the stories. Those big events aren't everyday occurrences. Most people, I feel, do pretty well in a crisis, but it's usually the little everyday things that get the best of us. Therefore, I think the biggest comeback or the biggest challenge that we all face is just managing our own emotions every day. Someone cuts us off in traffic; how are we going to respond? Our spouse doesn't do something we expect; how do we respond?

Something crashes at work; how do we respond to that? I think those are the biggest comebacks, the biggest challenges. It's the little things in life that I think keep most of us up at night, so I try to give people real-time practical strategies about how to deal with everyday life at home and at work. I would say that's the biggest challenge. Woody Allen said that ninety percent of success is just showing up. I think there's some truth to that.

Wright
When you consider the choices that you've made down through the years, has faith played an important role in your life?

Christopher
A very important role. I spend a lot of time in prayer and quiet time and silence. Spirituality is very important, especially in speaking, because you're in a position of people looking up to you and wanting to get something from you. I think if your heart's not in the right place, you're not going to have a very effective message. When I get up on stage, I want to be in the right frame of mind and the right heart and the right spirit, so I spend a lot of time doing that.

Wright
If you could have a platform and tell our audience something that you feel would help them or encourage them, what would you say to them?

Christopher
Some day I'm going to make up T-shirts with this statement on them: "Fail for it." We always hear "Go for it," but most successes and most inventions come out of previous failures. I always tell people to fail for it. Go ahead and take a risk, make a mistake. Don't be afraid of failure. Get out and try something stupid and see what happens. Learn from it and keep going.

Wright
We're down to the bottom of this half hour. I really do appreciate you being a guest on our program.

We have been talking to Bruce Christopher, who is considered America's foremost "Enter-Trainer." We have found out that he's also extremely intelligent and insightful.

Again, thank you for coming and talking to us on *Mission Possible!* today.

Christopher
It's a pleasure, David. Thank you.

About the Author

Laugh 'til you cry. Learn 'til you change. These are the only rules that apply at a Bruce Christopher presentation. What separates Bruce from the pack is his outrageously funny, dynamic delivery of today's hot topics. Bruce inspires audiences internationally by giving them real, immediate solutions for change without fluff and hype. Bruce has spoken at the prestigious Million Dollar Round Table Conference, London's Royal College of Surgeons, and the Mayo Clinic. He is a practicing supervising clinical psychologist, holding degrees in professional psychology and interpersonal communications. When organizations are faced with morale problems, communication conflicts, customer service issues, managing change, or teamwork issues . . . this psychologist is in!

Bruce Christopher
"Comedy With Content"
Psychologist and Humorist
(952) 988-9466 or (888) 887-8477
Fax: 952-945-7023
www.bcseminars.com

Chapter Eleven – Kevin Saunders

-

David Wright (Wright)

Today we're talking to Kevin Saunders, who was born and raised on a farm in the heartland of America. It was there that he learned at an early age that integrity and hard work are the keys to achievement. Kevin was injured in a 1981 grain elevator explosion in Corpus Christi, Texas, and was paralyzed from the chest down. The catastrophic blast destroyed the building in which he was working as a federal inspector, leaving ten coworkers dead. Doctors said he would not survive his injuries, but through courage, tenacity, and the will to live he beat the odds. He is an inspiration to those who, like himself, thrive on challenges and approach life with optimism, enthusiasm, and determination.

Kevin Saunders has received many awards, including a commendation from the President's Council on Physical Fitness, for outstanding contribution to physical fitness in sports. He was the first person with a disability to ever receive the American Association of Community Colleges Outstanding Alumnus of the Year award and the first individual with a disability appointed to the President's Council on Physical Fitness. He was appointed by President George Bush and re-appointed by President Bill Clinton. In fact, he's the only person who's ever been re-appointed. He's a professional speaker today and an author.

Kevin, it's an honor to have you with us on our program today.

Kevin Saunders (Saunders)

It's a real honor to be here.

Wright

Your life has a real *before* and *after*, doesn't it, Kevin?

Saunders

Yes, sir, it sure does.

Wright

Can you give our listeners and our readers a brief description of who Kevin Saunders was before the accident in 1981?

Saunders

I guess I was just a regular guy who graduated from college, got a job, went to work, and lived a normal life until that grain elevator explosion came my way.

Wright

That was on April 7, 1981. You were working as a federal inspector in Corpus Christi when the massive explosion erupted. Reporters from newspapers in Corpus Christi said "the blood and suffering were incomprehensible. Twisted and torn bodies squirmed unattended on concrete pavement." I can't even begin to imagine what this must have been like. Tell us what happened to you that day, Kevin.

Saunders

It was kind of a slow day. In fact, this was just the second day that I spent at that elevator. Having grown up in Kansas on the farm, I was going to take off the rest of that afternoon and go down to the ocean and do a little surfing on the Gulf of Mexico. But I decided to stick around and save my vacation time for later. In fact, I was doing some paperwork in the government lab right next to those big silos that are 30 feet around and 100 feet tall, stacked like cigarettes in a carton. I heard what sounded like a rumbling thunder and then an earthquake. It grew within fractions of a second to the point where the popping and cracking noise was so loud it felt like my head was going to split wide open. I looked up right through the window of that lab and saw the big walls of those concrete silos that are two feet thick blowing apart like they were paper. The ground was moving up and down a foot or two. I looked at my coworker, Albert Tripp, who was in the office with me, and he had a pale look on his face like we both knew that it was a grain elevator explosion. We knew that grain dust was more explosive than dynamite and gasoline and nuclear energy. You never think it's going to happen to you, but right then we knew it was happening. When you hear cracking and popping that loud, you know you're in serious trouble.

There wasn't time to go anywhere. There were six explosions that ripped through the grain elevator at 1,500 feet per second, each getting bigger and more powerful than the other, because it was knocking dust loose. The dust is what's explosive, not the grain. The more dust that got knocked loose, the bigger the explosions got. The building that I was in was completely destroyed. In fact, to show you how fate goes sometimes, my coworker, Albert Tripp, who was in his forties, hit the floor. I was just out of college, and I was standing there with a clipboard. The whole wall just literally blew out in my face. I was hurled three hundred feet over a two-story building and onto a concrete parking lot. When my body impacted that parking lot, my head and my shoulders hit. The neurosurgeon and the orthopedic surgeon said that my body flipped over and broke at the chest, and that collapsed my lungs, broke my scapulas, and left me with massive internal and external injuries. There were so many people out there that they ran out of stretchers in a town of 350,000 people. Thanks to one paramedic and the good Lord, I was placed onto a blown-off door, and that's the way I made it to the intensive care unit of Memorial Medical Center that day. I guess it wasn't my time to go.

Wright
People say there's a moment in a person's life after they've been told they're paralyzed in which the gravity of their situation really sinks in, and they have to choose a path, a mindset, an attitude, that will affect the rest of their life. Did you have a specific moment like that after the doctors told you the extent of your injuries?

Saunders
I was like most people when they are told that. I'd been involved in athletics in high school, and I played college football, track, rugby, and soccer at a varsity level. I was in denial. When you're told that you are paralyzed, you say, "You think I'm not going to walk? I'm going to walk out of this place." Finally you have to accept it. That's when depression enters in, when you finally realize that you have to accept the fact that you are paralyzed. Then you have to start trying to adjust to your new body, and that's quite a transformation. That's a bitter pill for anybody to swallow, whether you were a former athlete or not. I really enjoyed sports and was still playing rugby, racquetball, and working out at the health club, doing all those things right up to the day of the explosion. When I chose a path, it didn't come right at that particular time. It took me a while to work through the depression.

If you want to look at a point in time where my life took a direct turn, it was in the rehabilitation hospital. I rolled up behind a guy who was doing a painting. He said, "Hey, it's a great day, isn't it?" His name was Mick Davis. I said, "No, I think it stinks. What have you got to be happy about? You're in a wheelchair just like me in this rehabilitation hospital." He said, "Kevin, it's not what happens to you. It's how you respond to what happens." I guess I'd never looked at life like that. I figured there were a million things I could do before I got hurt and put in a wheelchair, and now there were probably only 999,000 things I could do. The guy who was drawing that picture— and it was an incredible drawing—was paralyzed from the neck down. He couldn't move anything but his head, but he was drawing everything, and even graduated from college, by holding a paintbrush or other tool in his teeth. While reading, he would turn the pages of a book with a thing with a stopper on it. You think you've got it tough; look around, and you'll always find somebody who's in a lot worse shape than you are, so make the best of what you've got.

Wright

Kevin, we're going to talk about some exciting and inspirational aspects of your life in a few minutes; however, things actually got a lot worse for you after the accident before they got better. You went through a bitter divorce. You lost a great deal of the settlement money through bad investments and to people who clearly didn't have your best interest in mind. You battled depression and substance abuse. What were those days like, and do you think the experience prepared you for the course your life has taken now?

Saunders

I came out of an injury that was so severe and so dramatic that my whole body had changed. It was hard for me just to sit up for very long periods at a time. When I was first released from the hospital, I was still in a body cast and still trying to get used to this new way of life and this new body that I was trying to live in. The newspaper told about the big settlement I was given, and people were beating down my door. The gal that I'd only been married to a few months before the accident told me she was pregnant when I got hurt. My son, Stephen, was born while I was in the hospital. She was knocking me out of my wheelchair, hitting me with things, throwing plates and glasses at me, and hitting me in the head with stuff because she was so frustrated because of what had happened to me. I think that's something people don't realize; she never tried any of that when I was a 6-foot, 200-pound guy who played college football. I think the kind of abuse that you see on TV on *Lifetime* and *Oxygen* might be reversed if it involved a male who didn't have the abilities and strength. And back then, I didn't have strength like I do now. I was trying to cope and get my life back, trying to mentally readjust.

I would see 70-year-old men crying because they were impotent, and there I was, paralyzed from the chest down, not able to move or feel anything. I had a bad situation happening. I had people coming to my door, wanting to do little favors for me, like screwing in a light bulb or sweeping up the floor. I'd offer to pay them, and they'd say no, they just wanted to help me. Then they'd come back and say they wanted thirty thousand dollars. They'd say, "What's thirty thousand to you? You've got millions, and you didn't have to work for it." Well, no, I didn't have to work for it, but I gave the use of my body from my chest down for the rest of my life.

In the state of Texas, the settlement was commingled property. How absurd! They later changed the law because of what happened to me. I should have gotten a partition in the funds, but I didn't think that was the right thing to do. For whatever reason, that's the way my life turned out. I want to believe people want to do the right thing. If you can't have trust and faith in people—I mean, you want to think that people will want to do what's right. If our society has decayed to the point where most people are out to take you every time you deal with them, we're getting into a sad state of affairs.

Wright

In your book titled *There's Always a Way,* you tell about your first experience as a wheelchair participant in a road race at the Peachtree 10K in Atlanta. It didn't turn out like you expected, but it was a turning point for you, wasn't it?

Saunders

Oh, absolutely! I showed up with my brother Joel. He and his family went and ran that road race. It's 10K, right down the middle of Peachtree Street in Atlanta, Georgia. Fifty thousand people run that race every year. It's the biggest 10K in the world, I believe. He said he'd seen athletes in wheelchairs racing there the year before. He asked me if I'd go, so I said sure. I showed up in my old hospital chair, you know, the big, old, clumsy, heavy wheelchair, sixty pounds. I'd been an athlete before I got hurt. I thought I could beat anybody. I was out of shape and just out of the hospital. When I got to the starting line, I saw these guys in wheelchairs that looked more like drag racers than wheelchairs. They looked at me and said, "Hey, buddy, you'd better get in your racer. It's almost time for the race to start." I grew up on the farm in Kansas, so I looked back at them and said, "Hey, I'm already in it." They just laughed at me. They fired the gun on the starting line and we took off. Before I knew it, I looked up and those guys and girls were almost out of sight. It was 6.2 miles, and I only had a pair of racquetball gloves on. Those guys had big, thick leather gloves like a rubber overshoe with padding in it. I had blisters when I got to mile four.

There was a 45-degree hill about three-quarters of a mile long. The sign at the bottom said Cardiac Hill. I looked at my hands, looked at that, and said, "No way." I think everybody gets to the bottom of the hill. We all have obstacles in life, and we want to give up sometimes. I guess for me that was one of them. We all need a little motivation to get past those obstacles. For me that day, the motivation was that they were playing some music on the side of the hill, the *Theme from Rocky*. I could see him drinking that glass full of raw eggs and beating that side of beef in the meat locker and breaking the ribs on it. I thought, If Rocky could do it, so can I. So I just cranked that old wheelchair and kept pushing. I had to inch up like an inchworm; if I let go of the push rims, I'd roll backwards. I got over that hill, and for the first time in my life I felt a sense of accomplishment, like I'd really done something and gotten past one of the big obstacles since my accident.

Then it was downhill toward the finish line and less than a mile to go. I guess I wasn't listening too closely, because a truckload of TV cameras and newspaper cameras came by, then Craig Virgin and Kip Keino, the top 10,000 meter runners in the world, came by. I'd seen them in the Olympics on TV. I thought, Hey, this is cool. I'm getting to run alongside two of the best 10K runners in the world. They had said at the beginning—and I didn't hear it—that they started the wheelchair athletes thirty minutes before the foot runners. If a foot runner passed a wheelchair runner, the wheelchair runner must immediately leave the racecourse. About that time, a great big lady with a Peachtree Road Race Official T-shirt came out there, grabbed hold of my shirt, and said, "Hey, you've got to get off the race course right now. You've been passed by a foot runner." I said, "No way, lady," and I pushed loose from her grip. I had gravity working for me, you know. I got a little distance between her and me and I thought, See ya at the finish line. I think that lady must have had some kind of radio communication device on her, because three more race officials that looked just like her set up a roadblock for me. They grabbed me and pulled me off the racecourse. I never made it to the finish line. I had tears come to my eyes, because I had never quit anything. That's the day I decided, and set a goal, that I was going to be one of the top wheelchair athletes in the world, and I was going to order one of those racing wheelchairs. I found out they had races in conjunction with the Olympic games for wheelchair athletes and people with disabilities. That's when I set a goal to bring back a medal from Seoul in 1988.

Wright

Kevin, you've used your success as a champion wheelchair athlete to encourage and inspire others. What are the primary lessons you try to communicate to people across America?

Saunders

What I try to communicate is that there's always a way. You've got to believe that you can always achieve something, and you never give up. Through courage, determination, and perseverance you can achieve things that you might not think are possible. That's when you discover the true capacity that you have. When you're really challenged, that's when you discover what capacity you really have. You have to be truly challenged—you have to be in a position where you *want* to do it or *have* to do it. If you're in that type of situation, then you can find capacities that you never even thought you had. I guess through all my time and through the divorce and all that I went through, I was driven. I didn't want to focus on all the negative aspects in my life.

My coaches had always said that I was a good, all-around athlete, if I applied myself. I had friends who went on and played pro football and became great athletes. Howard Cosell said about Paul Coffman, a friend of mine who played at K State, that he had to beg to try out with the Green Bay Packers. He not only made it on there, but he got drafted in the thirteenth round. He became an all-pro. There are stories of similar athletes who were all- Americans in track in college, guys that I beat in high school. The moral of the story is that there's no shortcut to success. It's good, old-fashioned hard work—and, of course, getting around other athletes that are the best at what they do so you can learn from them if you need to pick up your pace or learn some technique to help you improve. That's true in whatever you want to do. It's true for education or anything that you really want to do. If you want to be a great race car driver, get around the Andrettis or other people like that.

Wright

I've never met anyone with as much enthusiasm or as many exciting plans for the future as you have, Kevin. Could you tell our readers and our listeners a little about what lies ahead for you? I understand you've got an exciting project in the works.

Saunders

I was running to be the first person with a disability to chair the President's Council on Physical Fitness in Sports. Because of the 9/11 tragedy, the President's Council on Physical Fitness in Sports is really a unique entity. It's under the Department of Health and Human Services, which is headed by Secretary Tommy Thompson, and they're putting ninety percent of their time—just as President Bush said on the six-month anniversary—against the war on terrorism. That also goes for the Department of Health and Human Services, as far as the war on bio-terrorism and the health plan preparedness, the action plan. If they have an outbreak in a big city, they have the National Guard, the Red Cross. They are developing vaccines for polio and other diseases so they can be ready to combat this if it should happen to come to our country.

Rick Lewis, who designed the Husker Rack for Nebraska, played fullback at K State, and his little brother, Lance Lewis, was a three-year starter for Nebraska and was drafted by the Indianapolis Colts in 1993. Rick's bench press record was just broken by the guy on the football team who won the "Kevin Saunders Never Give Up Award" at Kansas State University. Rock Cartwright broke his bench press record for running backs at over 500 pounds. That's pretty good for a running back.

Anyway, Rick Lewis and I decided to carry on what Arnold Schwarzenegger had started by visiting all fifty states and the governors. Our goal is even more far-reaching, to get representatives from every school district in every state in the country to push my wheelchair in a marathon through key portions of every state. Our goal is to get a wide range of representatives, from inactive kids to elite blue chip athletes, to the presentations. I'll be doing 12.5 speaking engagements per week starting September 1 through May 31 for the next three years. For forty weeks per year I'll be getting in front of 2,500 to 5,000 people. I have a big trailer home from Kibbi

Motorhomes with a 24-foot living area and a 10-foot garage for racing chairs and hand-cranked cycles that I'll be using to push into each city. Then I'll be working out on some equipment that we'll take with us. We're going to be working with the NBA strength and conditioning coaches, the NFL Players Association, and Mark Verstegen and Adidas out of Phoenix. That's where Tiger Woods and Peyton Manning trained, as well as a lot of the top athletes out of college who are going into the NFL to get ready for the combines. We have access, depending on whatever time of year it is, to a famous person from some sport in each city. We're planning on kicking it off in San Antonio, Texas. We'll take a month to do Texas and probably less time to do a small state like Delaware. It will average out to two and a half weeks per state.

Wright

Most people are fascinated with the new television show about being a survivor. Do you think many people really understand their true potential for surviving and overcoming obstacles?

Saunders

I'd say that unless that's your field of study, you've really got to be there. You've just about got to be in a situation where you're knocking on death's door to really know what it's like. It's a pretty scary feeling when you hear cracking and popping around you. I understand a little bit better now what those guys in Viet Nam, who lived to tell about it, were probably feeling. After my accident, whenever somebody slammed a door or dropped a book, it shot up my spine (what I could feel) to the back of my head. It took me a couple of years to get over that. When the ground was going up and down a foot or two, I didn't think I'd see another day. Like I said, there was nothing left of the building I was in but the concrete foundation. God must have had His hand on me, and it wasn't my time to go.

Wright

Thank you for sending me a copy of your book, Kevin. I see it was endorsed by President George H. Bush, Senator Bob Dole, Arnold Schwarzenegger, Oprah Winfrey, and Dr. Robert Schuller. That's pretty heavyweight company.

Saunders

If I'd had a little more room I would have had a lot more testimonials. I should have put them on the inside pages! I've been real fortunate. I guess God had a plan for my life, and I think what I'm trying to do is fulfill that plan.

Wright

When you consider the choices that you've made down through the years and through all of your adversity, has faith played an important role in your life?

Saunders

Oh, absolutely! That's something important that I think you've got to have. Everybody who gets things accomplished in life, or everybody who gets it done very successfully, has got to believe in what they do. If you're going to achieve anything, you have to first believe. I think that the person is blessed who trusts in the Lord. You'll be planted by the river, and you'll grow roots that will spread far and wide. You'll be planted firm and stable and you will prosper.

Wright

Kevin, it has been a real pleasure talking to you today. Our time is over. Can you imagine thirty minutes has already gone by?

Saunders

Hey, time flies! That's why you've got to work hard, be the best you can be, and never, ever give up.

Wright

We have been talking to Kevin Saunders, who is, as all of us have found out, one great guy and a great professional speaker and author.

Kevin, it really has been an honor having you with us on our program today. I wish you all the success in the world.

Saunders

Thank you very much, David; it's been an honor to be on your show. Everybody have a great day . . . and never give up!

About the Author

Kevin Saunders travels nationwide motivating organizations, schools, associations, and Fortune 500 companies with his message to live a fit and healthy lifestyle. His passion is to educate, motivate and inspire through his Let's Roll On USA Tour. He inspires his listeners to realize that hard work and dedication can bring out the champion that lies within us all, and to never quit believing you can do anything if you "Never Give Up!" The heart of his message illustrates that it is not what happens to you that matters, but how you respond that makes all the difference.

Kevin Saunders
P.O. Box 7
Downs, KS 67437
(785) 454-3670
Fax: (785) 454-3674
Email: info@kevinsaunders.com
www.kevinsaunders.com

-

Chapter Twelve – Dr. Sandy Gluckman

-

David E. Wright (Wright)

Today we're talking with Sandy Gluckman, owner and president of The Gluckman Group. Dr. Gluckman has developed a unique approach to business transformation. Her training as a clinical psychologist and organizational developmental specialist gives her a deep understanding of the dynamics of change. Sandy has a Ph.D. from the University of Witwatersrand, South Africa, in the use of the whole brain in training and education, and has studied in the USA at the Adizes Institute for organizational growth and rejuvenation. Dr. Gluckman is an accomplished speaker and is in the process of publishing a book on a revolutionary third intelligence known as SQ, or intelligence of the Spirit.

Dr. Gluckman, welcome to *Mission Possible!*

Sandy Gluckman (Gluckman)

Thank you so much, David; I'm delighted to be here.

Wright

As I was reading your various publications and about the book you are working on, it occurred to me that there is a story behind the way your writings have evolved. Am I correct?

Gluckman

That is true, David; the book does reflect a journey I have been on, both personal as well as professional.

Wright

Is this something you would like to share with us?

Gluckman

Well, David, like everyone, my life has had its highs and lows, failures and successes, tragedies and joys. But if I look at the book I am writing and how I have evolved as a person as well as a professional, I would summarize my journey by saying that, first, I behaved as though I were only a logical, rational person who achieved excellent grades in all my studies. I was told that I had a high IQ! Everyone was so proud of my intellectual abilities. But something did not feel right for me, even though I led a successful life by most standards.

Second, I discovered that there was an entire part of my being that I had been denying, which was my emotional and creative self. What a discovery! This made me feel more whole as a person.

I discovered that at school I had been taught to be analytical, theoretical, logical, rational, and ordered in my thinking! Nobody was interested in my dreams, my fantasies, the products of my fertile imagination, my amazing intuition, or my dreams and feelings, so I had put them away. But actually these characteristics were a much stronger part of the true me than the logical part of me. This caused me to pursue a Ph.D. on becoming a whole person through using our intellect as well as our emotions, because rational logic and emotional logic are both forms of intelligence.

The third and probably most dramatic part of my journey was the discovery that there was yet another part of my being that I had been denying, the Spirit of who I truly am, the essential essence that is me, the utterly authentic part of me that is separate from the ego self I had created for society. I discovered that when I put my ego aside and allow my true Spirit to come forward, I am able to tap into an entirely new way of understanding and interpreting information. I discovered that the Spirit of who we are has an intelligence of its own that can transform information in a way that opens up opportunities and possibilities that we could not see before. That is why I have called this form of intelligence the intelligence of the Spirit, or SQ. I cannot even begin to describe what a huge difference this discovery is making to my life.

Wright

You write a great deal about the power of a vision, and it would seem that your journey has been inspired by your own vision. Would you share your personal vision with us?

Gluckman

Thank you for asking. I would love to achieve international acclaim for playing a significant role in putting Spirit and Soul back into organizations, in a way that produces enhanced profits. I have worked with organizations for twenty-eight years now and am shocked at what stultifying, mind-numbing, dispirited places organizations can be. My mission is to assist millions of people in reconnecting with the Spirit of who they are, so that they can liberate their true purpose and talent. I will do this by teaching them how to use the extraordinary intelligence of their Spirit (SQ) together with their IQ and EQ.

Wright

The concept of IQ has been around forever. EQ is relatively new.

Gluckman

Yes, for about ninety years we have recognized and measured only one form of overall intelligence, the intelligence quotient (IQ). Then in the 1990s the existence of emotional intelligence was brought to our attention by Goleman and others, and we are now recognizing the importance of this second form of intelligence, referred to as EQ. In my book, which is soon to be published, I suggest that it is now time to acknowledge a third form of intelligence, namely, the intelligence of the Spirit, referred to as SQ.

Wright

In a paper titled "Why Would You Need Change Management?" you state that your organization, The Gluckman Group, uses whole brain technology and whole brain tools in experiential planning and training workshops. Can you tell our listeners and readers what whole brain technology is?

Gluckman

Whole brain technology refers to thinking with both sides of the brain as opposed to a preference for thinking with only one side of the brain. Our brains have two parts, referred to as the left brain and the right brain, or left and right hemispheres. Each of these hemispheres receives and processes information differently. The left brain is logical, rational, analytical, theoretical. Language and numeracy are specializations of the left brain. When we think with the left brain, we will think in an ordered, sequential, detailed

The 2 Sides of the Brain

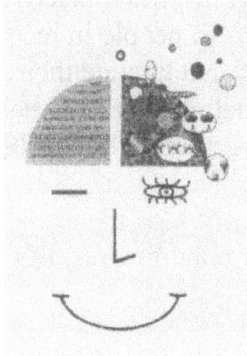

Left Brain	Right Brain
Linear	Lateral
Analytical	Imagination
Logical	Intuition
Theoretical	Creativity
Language	Emotions
Numbers	Storytelling
Sequential	Metaphor
Ordered	Motivational
Details	Perceptive
	The Big Picture

fashion. How we use this side of the brain will determine the level of our IQ.

The right brain, on the other hand, thinks creatively—so we will get an idea, feel emotion, intuitively know something, imagine an innovative new way. How we use this will determine the level of our EQ. With the right brain we create mental pictures that spark feelings. With the left brain we are able to plan how to implement the pictures we see.

But here comes the challenge: Each one of us is born with a preference for either left brain thinking or right brain thinking. There is a small percentage of the population who can use both hemispheres equally well, but most of us have a very definite inborn preference. This means we are born either left-brain dominant or right-brain dominant, and from that moment we will tend to receive, process, and transmit information from the preferred side of our brain far more often than from the other side.

What is YOUR preferred thinking style?

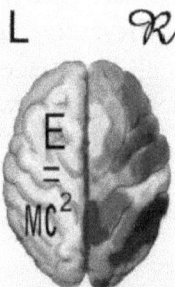

Are you Left brain dominant

The logical, rational, ordered planner?

Are you Right brain dominant

The intuitive, creative, new ideas, visionary?

A Balanced thinker?

If we respond to our world using mainly our preferred brain, this will result in "half-brained" thinking. When we know how to use the whole brain for planning, problem solving, and decision making, we will integrate the information from both sides, thus giving us a more comprehensive result . . . and a greater possibility of success.

But thinking with the less preferred brain is not comfortable. It does not feel natural. Please be aware, though, that I am not saying that because we have a preference for the thinking style of one side of the brain we do not ever use the other side. This is not so. We *will* use the less preferred side of the brain, but to a far lesser extent. Having an inborn preference simply means that thinking with the less preferred side does not feel so comfortable, and we will do this as little as possible unless we decide to consciously force ourselves to think with both sides. Particularly when we are under stress and pressure, we will automatically resort to thinking in the way that feels most comfortable for us.

Wright

So even though we have a natural, inborn propensity towards thinking with the one side, it is still possible to integrate the two?

Gluckman

Yes, it certainly is; in fact, it is highly desirable to do that, both in business as well as in our personal lives—it is the integration of the left and right brains that is referred to as *whole brain technology.*

Wright

So where does SQ fit in?

Gluckman

It has only very recently been discovered that SQ functions from the center of the brain and brings together the information from all our intelligences. Our brains are designed so that IQ, EQ, and SQ can work together or they can function separately. The ideal is for them to work together so that we can be the fully intellectual, emotional, and spiritual beings that we are.

Wright

Having studied music composition many years ago, I am a little confused. Music comes from the creative part of our brain, but I also know that music is mathematics. So is music a right brain or a left brain principle?

Gluckman

Well, that's a great question, because music beautifully played is a perfect example of the integration of the left hemisphere and the right hemisphere. Without the mathematical and theoretical abilities of the left brain, you would not be able to read the music. Without the emotion, imagination, intuition, and creativity of the right brain, you wouldn't be able to see the pictures created by the music. Music played theoretically perfectly, but devoid of feeling and imagination, is an example of using the left hemisphere alone. So if you put the ability to read and understand music together with the ability to add creativity and emotion to the music, you get an emotionally moving piece of music rather than music played in a possibly perfect, yet cold, theoretical manner.

Wright

So that would be the definition of *whole brain,* wouldn't it?

Gluckman

It would be a wonderful definition of whole brain.

Wright

Why is this of any importance to organizations?

Gluckman

Traditionally, business and even educational institutions—in fact, society in general—have emphasized the skills of the left brain only. The right brain was perceived as being somewhat "soft" and "flaky" and of little value in the serious corporate world. Now, for the first time since the industrial revolution, right brain thinking is receiving much recognition. It has become evident that the traditional ways of thinking have outlived their usefulness. A new respect is developing for the intuitive, imaginative, and visionary abilities of this side of the brain.

Think about it: Our greatest challenge in this new, harshly competitive business environment is to challenge our outdated assumptions and stereotypical perceptions and to be able to explore different perspectives. To thrive in this new economy we need to be able to think in a fundamentally different way.

The problem is that the rational, ordered left brain is not physiologically wired to think this way—it does not have the capacity to challenge outdated assumptions and outmoded business models; it cannot think radically differently. The right brain, on the other hand, does have the physiological capacity to do this. That is why organizations are now realizing that in order to achieve their highest goals, they must combine the logical, analytical side of the brain with the intuitive, creative side. This is the only way in which they can make plans and decisions that will be fundamentally different from what they did yesterday.

And thinking in a fundamentally different way is what will sort the winners from the losers.

Wright

Okay, assuming we agree with the logic of this, the question still remains: How do we make full use of the less preferred brain if we are not physiologically inclined that way?

Gluckman

The *first step* is to know what our own thinking style preference is. Being aware of this will alert us to what our personal thinking style could mean to us in terms of the kinds of decisions we will make in our lives. We actually have an excellent assessment tool that will tell you whether you are left brain or right brain dominant, whether you are an ideas person or a doer, what you will think about, and what you will leave out in your planning and decision making. When we use this with the executive team, they are fascinated by their personal and team profiles. They understand fully for the first time how they could be making absolutely biased (otherwise known as "half-brained") decisions.

The *second step* is to decide what we are going to do about this, based on the fact that whole brain thinking is superior to half brain thinking. Remember, the right brain provides us with intuitive and emotional logic. It is where our ideas come from. It is how we are able to see another way or envision the future or see the total picture. For right brain dominant people, thinking like this comes naturally, just as for left brain dominant people analysis, theory, concepts, finance, and details come naturally. *So what do right brain dominant people do when they need the information from the left brain . . . and vice versa?*

There are two options here. We can either learn how to integrate our own two brains, or we can team up with others who have the opposite preference. What I am actually saying is that either we learn to do this for ourselves by attending courses designed to teach us how to use more of our less preferred side of the brain and how to integrate the information from both sides, or we can identify those people in our personal lives, our teams, and departments who have a different way of thinking and incorporate them in our meetings and planning sessions and consciously include their differing perspective in our decisions. As long as we keep an open mind, they will assist us in thinking differently . . .and we will do the same for them.

This is tough, because our minds and our egos are inclined to want to deny this other reality. So in order to synergize the different perspectives of different types of thinkers, we need three characteristics . . .

an open mind,

little ego,

and a child-like curiosity.

We need to respect and be grateful for those people around us who think in a different way than we do.

Wright
I guess we all know what the tools of left brain thinking are, but what are the tools of right brain thinking?

Gluckman
Yes, the tools of the left brain, such as concepts, theories, balance sheets, budgets, reports, spreadsheets, statistical analysis, systems, processes, and project planning are tools that we are very familiar with. These thinking tools have been traditionally more accepted than those of the right brain. This is because in order to access the information from the right brain we have to use tools such as . . .

Brainstorming	Storytelling	
Mindmapping		Metaphor
Music	Theatre	Poetry
Drawing		Body movement
Videos	Collages	

You can imagine that such thinking tools have been regarded with much suspicion in the corporate world. Just look at how many decades people have been talking about a basic tool such as brainstorming and how little, even today, this superb tool is used in planning.

Wright

I can see why such tools would be shunned by business people—I guess they consider them to be frivolous. Could you give us some examples of how you use these tools?

Gluckman

By labeling these critical thinking tools as "frivolous," they are missing an opportunity to discover vital information that they need in their decision making and planning—information they cannot glean from being logical and rational.

For example, in our strategy sessions I will bring out piles of magazines, glue, scissors, and big project sheets, and ask executive teams to *create a picture collage of how they see the company in the future.* Some teams launch into this exercise with great glee, and these are the executives that have said to me, "Wow, I thought I had a clear vision of where this company is headed, until you gave me this blank project sheet and asked me to show you the vision. Then I realized I did not have a true vision in my mind's eye. Now I have a very clear vision—one that I can actually see." Other teams get locked into their negative prejudices about this kind of thinking process and look at me as though I have landed from another planet. And yet this is an excellent tool for adding another dimension to the process of envisioning the future and crafting innovative strategies. Today, though, this reticence to use the tools of the right brain is changing.

Wright

That's fascinating. What are some more ways in which you have used right brain thinking in strategic planning? And can such right brain tools be used for communication and perhaps for training?

Gluckman

Yes, to all of the above, David. We have all heard ad nauseam about how important good communication is. There is a very innovative and highly effective tool for corporate communication that I call *corporate theatre*. I am not referring to traditional roleplaying here; I am referring to actual theatre, using professional actors and professional scripts. We write the script that contains the message that leadership wants to get across, and it is acted out live to the organization.

Some leading-edge organizations are using theatre as a vibrant and very effective way of getting an important message across to thousands of employees. It is also being used as a training tool, because it brings life to otherwise boring training manuals. Most training is done mainly in a left brain way, which is extremely boring and mind-numbing. When training manuals are converted into theatre, this uses the intellect as well as the imagination and emotions of people. You would be amazed to see how people respond

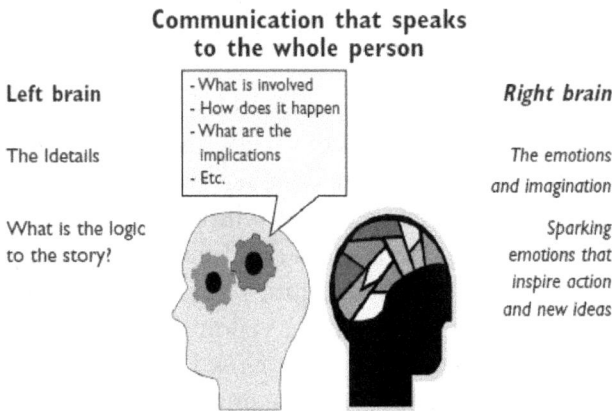

Communication that speaks to the whole person

Left brain

The Idetails

What is the logic to the story?

- What is involved
- How does it happen
- What are the implications
- Etc.

Right brain

The emotions and imagination

Sparking emotions that inspire action and new ideas

to communication through theatre—it is as though they come alive. And they never forget what they have seen, because they are responding with both sides of the brain—the logic and the feelings.

Another example of a right brain tool being used in strategy planning is the use of *"homemade" videos*. During strategy planning sessions, executives are split into small groups. Each team is given a video camera and several hours to create a video of what the organization will look like in the future. Each team then presents their video to the entire group. In this way they can actually "see" what their colleagues are thinking. The strategies that emerge are hugely superior to the kind of strategies that emerge from the traditional logic-only approach.

Music is also an excellent right brain tool that sparks innovative thinking. Imagine asking executives to select the music that symbolically represents the kind of culture they would like to create in the organization in the future. It is remarkable to see what insights this exercise can provide to the executives in their strategic planning sessions. For example, if some choose Beethoven's *Victory Symphony* and others choose a piece of laid-back jazz, obviously this will tell a very different story about the kind of organization they are seeing in their mind's eye.

These are just a few examples of right brain tools. Now, when we combine this kind of right brain thinking with the necessary analysis and theory of the left brain, we are using whole brain tools. *And the result is far superior to anything that can be achieved by using only one side of the brain.*

Wright
Is this what is often referred to as out-of-the-box thinking?

Gluckman
Great question, David! And yes, these examples are truly what out-of-the-box thinking is all about—thinking in ways that do not come natural to us. But our minds keep pulling us back to our preferred box, back to the way we have always thought. It is so easy to slip back into those deeply grooved neural pathways!

David, don't you wonder why so many executives of so many companies go on executive retreats simply to reiterate what they believe rather than to discover different perspectives? After all, you would think it is common sense to suggest that an executive team should challenge their own assumptions before making critical decisions. Well, I guess they do this because they do not know how to get out of the box, and they actually often do not want to know how to think outside of their own box, because it feels too challenging and uncomfortable. And above all, their egos have convinced them that they have all the answers. So they create jokes that deride the value and purpose of the concept of out-of-the-box thinking, and they self-righteously stay in their box.

Personal Baggage

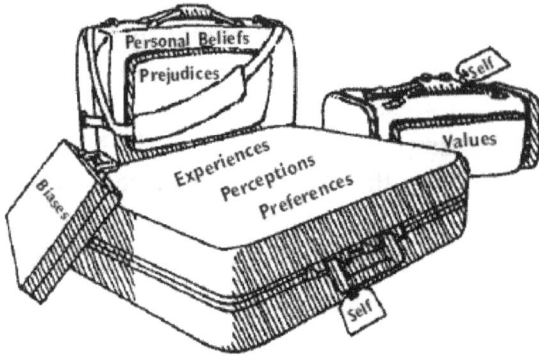

"The significant problems we face cannot be
solved at the same level of thinking we
used when we created them."

— Albert Einstein

Wright

Does this mean that decision makers should hire a consultant who does not think like they do, someone with a clearly different thinking style to what is the norm in the company?

Gluckman

Most definitely! But what are the chances of this happening? I know from my own experience that when prospective clients interview me, they are really wanting to assure themselves that I will think like they do. If they get the feeling that I am "not like them," some will not hire me. They hire someone who thinks like them, and then they proceed to spend many, many hours validating their thoughts inside their personal and corporate boxes. Groupthink like this is death to thinking out of the box. The result? They create a vision and strategies that are simply minor tweaks of what they did the previous years . . . and when they implement this, they find that the strategy is not innovative enough to assist them in outsmarting the competitors, making themselves more relevant to the marketplace, enhancing revenue, or creating improved shareholder value. Had they been able to think outside of their box, they would have discovered a whole new direction and purpose for the company; they would have created a new business model that represents a creative and financially superior alternative for the organization.

Wright

So now I understand about left brain and right brain intelligence, or IQ and EQ. We touched on SQ earlier. I read with interest the first few chapters of your book that's soon to be published. Could you tell our listeners more about this fascinating form of intelligence and how it is different from IQ and EQ?

Gluckman

The most profound difference is that the intelligence of both IQ and EQ are finite. The intelligence of the Spirit is infinite. What this means is that IQ and EQ are bound by neurological restrictions that limit what we can do with the information that we have.

With IQ and EQ we can only interpret the information and find new ideas within the boundaries of our past experience and knowledge. SQ has the capacity to go beyond our programmed selves, to transcend the IQ and EQ boundaries and go beyond the limits of our knowledge, perceptions, beliefs, and feelings in order to put the information into a wider context. Instead of being locked into finite thinking, we can now think in infinite terms. When we use SQ, we are able to synthesize the rational information from IQ and the emotional information from EQ and place it into a far wider context that has no boundaries.

SQ
The Intelligence of the Spirit

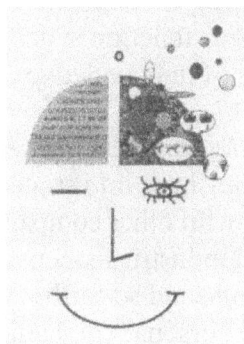

IQ		EQ
Left Brain		**Right Brain**
Linear		Imagination
Mechanical		Fantasy
Analytical		Artistic Ability
Logical		Intuition
Routine Memory		Creativity
Verbal		Emotion
Reading		"Gestalt"
Writing		The Big Picture
Arithmetic		

When we do this, the information is transformed in a way that makes many more things possible. This broader interpretation enables us to see extraordinary opportunities and possibilities. Only SQ is neurologically capable of this. This is immensely exciting and has profound implications for personal and organizational growth.

Let me give you some examples of these extraordinary SQ aptitudes that go beyond IQ and EQ. IQ and EQ can only work with one reality at a time, so these forms of intelligence split everything into . . .

right or wrong

good or bad

black or white

This limits us. With SQ, on the other hand, we are able to transcend this kind of "either-or" thinking. SQ has the ability to *synthesize many realities*, many seemingly contradictory perspectives, many ideas, and create something better. SQ can grasp *the interconnectedness of all things*.

Twenty years ago the U.S. auto industry was stuck with an either-or. They offered customers either quality or low cost. Toyota offers both. The airline industry said we could have either the lowest fares or the highest customer satisfaction. Southwest delivers both . . . and very creatively!

With IQ and EQ we are able to intellectualize and imagine such critically important concepts as authenticity, values, synergy, interdependence, vision, humility, and intuition, but IQ and EQ will empower us to authentically walk the talk. With SQ we don't talk about these concepts, *we become them . . . we are them*. When we have SQ, we behave according to our deepest authentic values. We feel true humility. It comes naturally to us to function synergistically and interdependently. We see visions of unbounded greatness and know that anything is possible.

With SQ we grasp the *boundarylessness and the interdependence of all things*. For example, this translates into strategic alliances, forging partnering arrangements with other companies, services, and products—in related or unrelated industries—networking globally, being aware of synchronous events, and so forth.

With SQ we experience true personal epiphanies and true mind shifts. We have these amazing "Aha!" experiences.

SQ gives us the capacity to understand and benefit from *the marvelous concept of synchronicity*. We are able to recognize it when it happens and use it in a way that has great meaning and purpose. This means that we are able to see the panoramic view of things, and when something happens in our lives, we are able to see how it could fit into the grand scheme. *We think in wholes rather than in parts. We operate with a mindset of abundance rather than scarcity, and we can hear and listen to the wisdom of our inner voice.*

Wright

Most mission statements I have read on the walls of organizations seem to have been crafted by a wordsmith and sound a little too much like advertising copy to me. How important is a mission statement for a company that truly wants to follow good business principles?

Gluckman

I would say that a mission statement is probably one of the most important elements of any company. It is actually the centrifugal force that holds the entire company together. The mission statement becomes the guiding light for all goal setting, role clarification, for all decision making, and for all measurement. It is the statement that articulates how the company intends to stand head and shoulders above others in the industry and what it will be known for doing with great mastery. The mission statement describes what the competitive edge of the company is. The mission statement becomes the basis for branding and marketing. So yes, I see a mission statement as an absolutely critical business principle.

Of course, there are mission statements . . . and then there are mission statements. A great mission statement is one that is eight words or less and that succinctly and clearly defines what the company does that makes it unique in the marketplace.

Let's look at what a good mission statement sounds like. Many years ago, Apple's mission statement was . . .

"A computer for every man, woman and child."

That is a great statement: concise, inspiring, and measurable. British Airways is also a good example . . .

"To become the world's favorite airline."

In 1993 they won the award for the most profitable airline in the world.

Here is an example of an uninspiring mission taken from the website of an organization (to be unnamed) . . .

"We support the President, the National Security Council, and all who make and execute U.S. national security policy by:

- **Providing accurate, evidence-based, comprehensive, and timely foreign intelligence related to national security; and**
- **Conducting counterintelligence activities, special activities, and other functions related to foreign intelligence and national security as directed by the President."**

I guess you can see why this mission statement may be considered one that would not inspire great performance. You know, David, the whole issue of IQ, EQ and now SQ—or left brain, right brain, and Spirit—comes into play here. Some leaders who are mainly left hemisphere dominant cannot see the purpose of a vision statement or a mission statement. They do not want one, and if they have one they do not understand how to "operationalize" this.

Leaders who can integrate left and right brain—IQ and EQ—will intuitively understand the value of a mission statement; they will create one that they feel emotionally inspired by, they will use it as a motivational tool, and they will measure it in dollars. This is good, but it is still not good enough if companies are going to thrive in this new economy. Leaders with high SQ will be able to see opportunities inherent in the mission that we cannot envision using only IQ and EQ, because with SQ they think in infinite terms rather than finite terms. They are not restricted by the space, time, and form boundaries of IQ and EQ.

Wright
Give us some more examples of companies that display SQ in their thinking.

Gluckman
One way to answer this is to look at who is weathering the recession the best. **Dell**, **Southwest**, and **WalMart** have created radical innovation to traditional cost structure, and they are getting better results than most other companies. Dell could still have been focusing on dealer strategies, but they questioned the business model. How did Southwest question the traditional ticketing and routing? They could still be looking for the best strategies within the old model, but they broke the mold. The result? Southwest, which is barely a generation old, now has a market value that is greater than the next five airlines combined.

Wright

Dr. Gluckman, let me quote something that you have written: "The ability to create and implement innovative strategies lies at the heart of the achievement of any successful company's vision." Could you define what you mean by innovative strategies?

Gluckman

An innovative strategy is one in which new and novel ideas have been introduced, resulting in a strategy that is groundbreaking and modern, pioneering a new line of thought.

It is a strategy that is the product of fundamentally different thinking, where the executives have arrived at new and novel conclusions based on their agreement that conventional wisdom is inadequate. Innovative strategies include concepts of interdependency, boundarylessness, synchronicity, and holism. Actually there are two aspects to identifying whether a strategy could be called innovative or not. The first is the process used to create it, and the second is the product itself. If someone were to say to me, "We have an innovative strategy," this is what I would ask before I would ask to see the strategy . . .

"Tell me how you created the strategy. What was the process?
Who was there? What was the climate in the room?
How did people behave?"

If they were to describe a strategy session where the delegates represented a good mix of different personalities and thinking styles, where there was strong mutual trust and respect, where they had the capacity to challenge their own and each other's assumptions and beliefs, where there was a climate of open dissent and heated debate, where people were comfortable with clashing viewpoints and challenging questions—then I would say, "Let me hear about your strategy; there is a good chance that it is indeed innovative."

Wright

Do you have examples of companies whose strategies are innovative and indicate SQ thinking?

Gluckman

A great example of this is what **Swatch** did. They were being left behind by their Japanese competitors. They realized they had to do something different, so they married Swiss watch making skills with Italian fashion design, and then borrowed plastic engineering skills from Lego to produce watches that were dramatically different from Casio, Citizen, and Seiko. This kind of thinking breaks boundaries.

Sony is another example. Their single most profitable business is PlayStation. It is interesting, though, that Ken Kutaragi, who invented this, had to fight the system for years until eventually he found a senior executive who would sponsor his idea. He had to find one other person with SQ. Everyone else could not extend their thinking beyond their IQ and EQ to see the possibilities.

Wright
Do you have any examples of companies that have missed the boat because of a lack of SQ in their strategizing?

Gluckman
Think about **Coca-Cola.** Coca-Cola missed some of the most important beverage trends in the past twenty years: late going into fruit flavored teas—Snapple did this first; late going into sports drinks— Gatorade did this first; late going into designer water—Nestle is number one in the world in that business; late going into New Age beverages, and far behind companies such as Red Bull. How could Coca-Cola miss these trends? No SQ. They were a prisoner of their IQ and EQ thinking, which kept them prisoner to their traditional business model.

Wright
Is this why some people see opportunities and others don't? How do the radical innovators look at the world? Do they do this with SQ?

Gluckman
Yes, they look at the world through a different lens—the lens of SQ. When you use IQ and EQ to think about the future, you will be stuck with seeing things as they are and have been. With IQ and EQ we cannot challenge beliefs that we have always taken for granted; we cannot ask the stupid questions that no one else has asked nor see the unlimited possibilities that others cannot see.

Wright

So why do we not use these skills? It sounds like this kind of intelligence is available to us all, but we don't all know how to use it. Is this correct?

Gluckman

That is exactly right! And the reason why we cannot all tap into our own SQ is because *our ego gets in the way*. Each one of us has an authentic self and an ego self. Although we are born utterly authentic and Spirited, we soon learn that to get the approval of others we have to be what they want us to be, so we hide our true Spirit and develop a persona called the ego. The task of the ego is to obtain approval from others and to protect us from uncomfortable challenge and emotional pain. To do this, the ego must keep us away from our true Spirit, and that is why we cannot use the intelligence of our Spirit. When the ego is in control, we can *only* use the intelligence of IQ and EQ—and then *only to a limited degree*. So to tap into the intelligence of the spirit, we have to first minimize the power of the ego and reconnect with the being behind the ego, which is our true Spirit. When we are loyal to our true Spirit, we will tap into an intelligence that offers us capabilities which are far superior to IQ and EQ.

Wright

In your book, you write about *I-ness* and *we-ness*. I'm not sure what you mean. Could you give me an explanation or an example?

Gluckman

I-ness is an authentic state of being in which I am I. I am not my ego self. I am my real self. I am my true Spirit. In other words, the power of the ego personality has been minimized and replaced by the authentic Spirit that defines who I truly am.

Now let's look at the concept of *we-ness*. A strange thing happens as we strengthen our I-ness: We begin to understand how small we are in the bigger scheme of things and how little real power we have to make a meaningful difference without the full support of others. This may sound like a contradiction in terms, but it's not really. The paradox is that you cannot realize how *powerless* you are without others until you realize how *powerful* you really are personally. Only when you become aware of your own personal power are you able to feel humility. So true humility is a consequence of I-ness. It is this humility that creates we-ness, which is the respectful, meaningful, and synergistic connection with others.

Wright
How would we go about creating or strengthening our own I-ness and we-ness if we wanted to do this?

Gluckman
We must first learn how to distinguish between . . .

> "the real me"
> and
> "the not real me."

To do this, we must confront the illusions and lies of the ego. We need to be able to grasp the truth that all events or characteristics or people are neutral until our ego imposes a positive or negative interpretation on them. We must take ownership of the fact that every one of us is made up of every characteristic that constitutes man—and in equal proportions. We are equally . . .

> good and bad
> wonderful and terrible
> right and wrong
> smart and stupid
> caring and uncaring
> and . . . and . . . and!

We are not a combination of selected positive characteristics only . . .

> We possess them all.

Granted, some appear to be more visible and prominent than others; but the truth is that every time I do something really smart or caring or creative, I am also doing something equally stupid, uncaring, and uncreative, somewhere, with someone in my life.

When we are able to open our minds to this information and acknowledge that we do indeed possess every single aspect of human nature in ourselves, we will neutralize the ego and reconnect with our Spirit and its enlightened intelligence.

We cannot connect with our SQ when our ego is denying half of our being.

By accepting this truth, we are able to let go of the illusions of the ego and the labels of the ego. So to answer your question, David, this is why we cannot automatically use our third intelligence; we first need to acquire the ability to liberate this intelligence.

Wright
Dr. Gluckman, with our *Mission Possible!* talk show and book, we're trying to encourage people in our audience to be better, to live better, and to be more fulfilled by listening to the examples of our guests. Is there anything or anyone in your life that has made a difference for you and helped you to become a better person?

Gluckman
I am thinking about your term "a better person," and I would just like to say that I sincerely hope that I am a better person today than I was yesterday, and that I will be even a better person tomorrow. So for me, becoming a better person is a moving target and a lifelong journey. There are times when this journey seems too much or feels overwhelming, and then the one thing that helps me to keep going is the fact that I know what my personal purpose is; I am driven by a vision for myself, a vision that inspires me to keep reaching higher and higher.

I believe that nothing happens without a reason. The universe has a grand plan, and when I connect my personal purpose with the energy of the universe, I am capable of great things. With the help of some very special mentors, I have learned how to do this. I have learned that when I allow the tyranny of my ego to take control, I am lost, so I am constantly working at recognizing the games of my ego and minimizing the power of the ego . . . and replacing this with the humility and courage that I find when I am authentic. All I can tell you is that it is a most amazing feeling when I am able to stay connected to my Spirit and purpose. I have watched what happens. When I am being true to myself, and to my purpose, the right people come into my life, doors open to assist me with my dreams, and I am able to envision the most creative possibilities. The one thing that makes this all possible is the courage to look at myself and to challenge my assumptions about who I am.

Wright

What do you think makes a good mentor? In other words, are there characteristics that mentors seem to have in common?

Gluckman

I would say that there are three major characteristics that great mentors have in common . . .

The first is personal authenticity,
the second is personal authenticity,
and the third is personal authenticity!

Seriously, I would be gravely concerned about a mentor who has not been through some soul searching. I would venture to say that great mentors are people who been through their own tragedies or failures and have risen above these to discover their own unique strengths and talents, and who, in the process, have been able to put their ego away. Great mentors are role models of what they teach, and their teachings are clearly reflected in their behavior. In this way their students learn by watching as well as by listening—by seeing the words in action.

Wright

Most people in our culture are fascinated by these new television shows about being a survivor. What has been the greatest comeback that you have made from adversity in your career or in your life?

Gluckman

My beautiful, vital 21-year-old daughter died of a virulent form of meningitis. One minute she was there, and the next she was gone forever. Only a parent who has lost a child can know how soul destroying and devastating this can be. From that terrible moment on, nothing is ever the same again. Every minute of every day is filled with such immense pain that you wonder how you are ever going to make it through that day without seeing your beloved child again. Nothing else matters. It feels as if there is a big, black gaping hole inside of me. Because her death was so totally unexpected, I was in a state of shock for many, many years. I know that the healing process will be one that will continue for the rest of my life. I doubt that a parent ever gets over the death of a child, but I am grateful for all the wonderful things that my daughter taught me.

Wright
So from adversity one draws strength?

Gluckman
It has been like that for me.

Wright
When you consider the choices you've made down throughout the years, has faith played an important role in your life?

Gluckman
That is an interesting question. In some ways I would say definitely yes, it has . . . but only up to a point. I believe that faith can be a stumbling block or it can be a stepping-stone. Let me explain why I say this. We need to have faith when there is uncertainty, when there is an unknown. Uncertainty is accompanied by fear, and hence the need to have faith.

But uncertainty is replaced by certainty when two things happen. First, living our lives driven by an inspiring vision we have for ourselves gives us clarity of purpose. It gives us certainty. Second, when we grasp in the deepest way possible that over and above all the chaos our egos create for ourselves, there lies a hidden harmony, or a divine order. When we have this kind of certainty, we no longer need faith. So that is why I say that faith has played a part in my life, but only as a stepping-stone whenever I needed to move from uncertainty and fear to certainty and love.

Wright
If you could have a platform and tell our audience something that could help them and encourage them, what would you say?

Gluckman
I would ask the audience to think about this: When the voice and vision on the inside is greater than the voices and opinions on the outside, we have mastered our lives. What I mean by this is that I

believe that every one of us is born with a personal vision or purpose that we are meant to fulfill. We just need to find this inside ourselves. I love to quote Michelangelo. When he was asked how he created the statue of David, he said,

> **"I saw the angel in the marble,**
> **and I chiselled until I set it free."**

I would encourage the members of our audience to honor the true and authentic Spirit of who they are, because then they will see their own angel in the marble and life will take on a whole new meaning.

Wright

Dr. Gluckman, I really appreciate your being with us today. You have some brilliant concepts, and I'll bet our listeners are wondering how to get in touch with you and talk to you personally. It has been very, very interesting. Thank you so much.

Gluckman

Thank you, David, and I appreciate being able to talk to you and share this with you and your listeners.

Wright

Today we have been talking to Dr. Sandy Gluckman, owner and president of The Gluckman Group. She is a clinical psychologist and a great author with great ideas that I have really been fascinated with here today.

Again, we thank you so much for being with us.

Gluckman

Thank you, David.

About the Author

   Dr. Sandy Gluckman is a master strategist who works with business leaders worldwide. Her Ph.D. in "whole brain" thinking and her postgraduate studies in organizational growth are the basis of her uniquely different approach to the development of people and companies. She is an artist in tapping into the latent abilities of an organization and its people, and assisting organizations in creating innovative changes that result in enhanced profit. Her tested and highly innovative methodology and tools have been used in organizations in the USA, France, England, Germany, Australia, and South Africa. She is also a sought-after keynote speaker at leading international conferences, and is recognized as being a speaker with a difference because of the inclusion of theatre and music in her presentation.

Dr. Sandy Gluckman
3920 Sundew Court
Plano, TX 75093
(972) 758-1246
Fax: (972) 758-7837
Mobile: (214) 682-8980
E-mail sandy@gluckmangroup.com
www.gluckmangroup.com

Book Dr. Libhart to speak at your next meeting or event.

Radio/Television personality and author, she is a sought-after motivational speaker. Conducting workshops and seminars in family relationships and professional etiquette worldwide. Inducted into the Oxford Graduate School of Society Scholars, Dr. Libhart takes pleasure in travel, hard work, and lending her unique skills to those in need around the globe.

Growing and Going!

Dr. Libhart conducts her presentations for groups of small business owners, churches, and others who wish to learn about overcoming tasks and making life's missions possible. Depending on your format, time available, and meeting objectives, her presentations can run from thirty minutes to a few days. Zeroing in on the core issues people face on a daily basis!

For availability and booking information contact Dr. Libhart at 877-823-6886 or drbonnie@me.com.

www.DrBonnieL.com

Final Thoughts

1. Share *Mission Possible!* with your friends, family members, and colleagues. Buy 50 copies and receive a 50% discount off of the retail price. Call (877) 823-6886 for special pricing on larger quantities.

2. **Send us your comments**. We'd like to hear your success stories, insights, and any ideas you have for our future reference and additional books. Mail or send an e-mail to:

    > Dr. Bonnie Libhart
    > Hart & Taylor Media
    > 29 Braxton St.
    > Huntsville, AL 35806
    > DrBonnie@me.com

3. **It Takes Two!** Thank you to all of my friends, my family, my book team, my clients, and my colleagues in the National Speakers Association. Your faith in me and support of my work has surpassed my wildest dreams.

    Dr. Bonnie Libhart

www.ingramcontent.com/pod-product-compliance
Lightning Source LLC
Chambersburg PA
CBHW050106210326
41519CB00015BA/3847